Encouragement
FOR WHEN
Life is Hard

Encouragement
FOR WHEN
Life is Hard

Comforting Devotions
for a Woman's Heart

Renae Brumbaugh Green

BARBOUR
PUBLISHING

© 2018 by Barbour Publishing, Inc.

ISBN 978-1-63609-390-1

Adobe Digital Edition (.epub) 978-1-63609-540-0

Published by Barbour Publishing, Inc., 1810 Barbour Drive, Uhrichsville, Ohio 44683, www.barbourbooks.com

Our mission is to inspire the world with the life-changing message of the Bible.

Member of the
Evangelical Christian
Publishers Association

Printed in China.

GOD'S WAY IS PERFECT

As for God, his way is perfect: the LORD's word is
flawless; he shields all who take refuge in him.

PSALM 18:30 NIV

God's way is perfect. That sounds nice. . .but it also sounds a little cliché, especially when we're in the throes of heartache and despair. If God's way is perfect, why does it hurt so much? Is God cruel? Doesn't He care about us?

God's way is without flaw. . .but life has plenty of imperfections and shortcomings. As long as we're on this earth, we will have trouble. Didn't He say as much? But when we run to Him in that trouble, He is a shield. He is a refuge. He is our safe place. When we run to Him, He will love us, comfort us, and protect us. Life may not be perfect, but God always is.

Dear Father, thank You for Your perfect love.
Remind me, when life is hard, that I can run to You.
Thank You for always being there for me. Amen.

A MIGHTY WARRIOR

"The LORD your God is with you, the Mighty
Warrior who saves. He will take great delight
in you; in his love he will no longer rebuke
you, but will rejoice over you with singing."
ZEPHANIAH 3:17 NIV

Anxiety is defined as stress or uneasiness of mind caused by fear of danger or misfortune. Certainly this life is fraught with danger and misfortune. When we walk through our days without God, we have every reason to be afraid. But we don't have to travel this journey alone! We have a bodyguard—as well as a spirit guard—who will never leave us nor forsake us. He is the mighty warrior who saves!

He takes great delight in those who love Him and stay close to Him. Surely we have nothing to fear with a hero who adores us. He loves us beyond description. He will protect us and save us. With God as our defender, we have no reason to feel afraid.

Dear Father, thank You for being the
mighty warrior who saves. Remind me of Your
presence, and help me not feel afraid. Amen.

HARD WORK

Whatever you do, work at it with all your heart,
as working for the Lord, not for human masters.

COLOSSIANS 3:23 NIV

Work can be a drudge or a delight—depending on
the day, depending on the circumstance. When we
find ourselves in a job that fits our gifts and talents
and working for people who appreciate us, work
gives us immense satisfaction. But when we are in a
job that doesn't fit our personalities or our skills, or
when we work with people who take us for granted,
it can feel like a never-ending prison sentence.

No matter what type of job we're in, God wants
us to remember we're really working for Him. He will
bless honesty, diligence, and a respectful attitude.
We can pray for better opportunities and acquire
the skills to move us to a new position. In the meantime, we need to remember our *real* boss is loving
and generous, and He will reward us for hard work.

Dear Father, help me find satisfaction in my
job. I want to honor You in my work. Amen.

GOD'S PLAN

If you pay attention to these laws and
are careful to follow them. . .the LORD
will keep you free from every disease.

DEUTERONOMY 7:12, 15 NIV

This entire passage lists ways in which God will bless those who live righteous, upright lives. Keeping us free from disease is just one of the ways God blesses the godly. Yet we all know godly people who are afflicted with some sort of terrible disease. So does God not keep His promises?

Of course He does. As long as we are in this world, we will never be entirely immune. However, living clean, upright lives does lead to a healthier existence. We are less likely to get cancer if we don't put bad things into our bodies. We are less likely to get STDs if we follow God's guidelines for sex within marriage. God's laws are put in place because they're good laws, and they bring about health and longevity. Even when disease does strike, righteousness still produces the abundant life that cannot be found outside God's plan.

Dear Father, thank You for Your perfect
guidelines for healthy, righteous
living. Please heal me. Amen.

GOD'S PROMISE

"The LORD himself goes before you and will be with you; he will never leave you nor forsake you. Do not be afraid; do not be discouraged."

DEUTERONOMY 31:8 NIV

God promised to never leave us nor forsake us. He is eternal, so He's already been to the future and back. He goes before us, smoothing the path, preparing the way. When we walk with God, we have nothing to fear.

Others in our lives may have failed in their promises to stand by us, but God cannot fail. He will never break a single vow; it's not in His nature. When we feel alone, we can remind ourselves that we're never alone. Breathe in His presence, for He is right there. When we fear the future, remember He knows what's ahead, and He will walk with us every step of the way. God promised to stay with us and take care of us, and He always keeps His promises.

Dear Father, thank You for Your promise to stay with me and care for me. I feel Your presence, and I know You're here. Amen.

GOD HEARS OUR CRIES

May the LORD answer you when you are in distress;
may the name of the God of Jacob protect you.

PSALM 20:1 NIV

We humans can be odd creatures. In all of nature, we're the only ones who hide our distress behind a smile. We hold our chins up and our shoulders back and press on, never letting on that behind our confident exterior, we're crumbling.

But God hears the cries of our hearts! He knows our suffering and feels our sorrow. When we call out to Him—even if through a silent seeping of our emotions, hidden behind the safety of our poised facade—He will answer! He loves us, and He will never leave us to trudge through troubled times alone.

There is never a need to hide our heartache from God. He sees us at our worst, and He thinks we are magnificent! He adores us. Whatever our source of distress, He knows. He cares. And He is there.

> *Dear Father, thank You for hearing the cries*
> *of my heart. I'm going through a hard time*
> *right now. I need to feel Your presence in my*
> *life; I need You to rescue me. Amen.*

WITHOUT A DOUBT

*Now faith is confidence in what we hope for
and assurance about what we do not see.*

HEBREWS 11:1 NIV

Seeing is believing. At least that's what the world tells us. But God's ways are not our ways. God wants us to believe *before* we see. He wants us to be so certain of what we hope for that we don't even question the reality of it. After all, He calls us to a life of faith. Belief, after the fact, isn't really faith at all. It's just acknowledgment of something that has already happened.

Satan wants us to question our faith or belief in the good God has in store for us. He whispers lies into our spirits. He tells us it's never gonna happen. If he can shake us at the core of our faith, we're giving Satan exactly what he wants.

But just as God promised Noah He would send a flood, just as surely as God told Abraham He would provide an heir. . .we can *know*, without doubt, that God will honor His promises to us. And His promises include such good things beyond what we can imagine.

Dear Father, I believe. Amen.

GOD'S FAVOR

May the favor of the Lord our God rest on us;
establish the work of our hands for us—
yes, establish the work of our hands.

PSALM 90:17 NIV

God designed work to be an immensely satisfying activity. Hard work may not be fun, but it does give us a sense of purpose, helps us pay the bills, and helps us sleep well at night. When we feel our work isn't making a difference, it can cause us to question our existence.

We all go through periods of dissatisfaction with our jobs. But when we go for long periods without finding joy or purpose in our work, we should ask God for wisdom. Perhaps we need to change jobs. Perhaps we need to change our attitudes. When we pray about our jobs, we should make sure we're pleasing God with our efforts. Then we can ask for His favor to rest on us and trust that He will establish and bless our work.

Dear Father, may Your favor rest upon me in my job. Establish the work of my hands. Amen.

GODLY LEADERS

Then the LORD raised up judges who delivered them
from the hands of those who plundered them.
JUDGES 2:16 NASB

Have you ever stood inside the voting booth with no clue which person to vote for? Have you ever wondered, in despair, if there is a single person who is both capable and willing to serve our country with sincere ethics and political skill? God's Word tells us not to worry. God will raise up the leaders He wants to use in His perfect timing.

When the Israelites were being plundered, they probably felt like God had forgotten them. But He hadn't forgotten. God will never, ever forget those who call Him by name. In His time, He brought forth judges to deliver Israel from evil hands. In His time, He will raise up godly leaders who will deliver His children from those who use their power for personal gain at the expense of the needy and helpless.

When all hope seems lost, we can remember the Israelites, and remind ourselves that God's got it all under control.

Dear Father, I trust You to bring up godly
leaders. Please do it soon. Amen.

GENEROUS PROVIDER

*But if anyone does not provide for his relatives,
and especially for members of his household, he has
denied the faith and is worse than an unbeliever.*

1 TIMOTHY 5:8 ESV

One of the reasons God created the family system is so we wouldn't be alone. It has always been God's plan—by His design—that we rely on our families during difficult times. But modern society encourages a look-out-for-number-one mentality. We often feel burdened and resentful when we are asked to help out a family member in need.

When we have opportunity to help out a relative, we should see it as a privilege, not a drain. At those times, we have the chance to step into God's shoes for just a moment. He is a generous, loving provider, and He never turns His back on His children. By becoming a generous, loving provider for someone else, we become like God, or godly. And God always blesses those who try to be like Him.

*Dear Father, teach me to be a generous, loving
provider for the people in my family. Amen.*

ON BORROWING MONEY

The rich rule over the poor, and the borrower is the slave of the lender.

PROVERBS 22:7 NRSV

Money lenders can be slick operators. Credit companies often don't care if you can afford something or not. They want to loan you money because they know they'll get it back with exorbitant interest. That's why the Bible cautions against borrowing money unless it's absolutely necessary.

Instead of buying a new car, we can often buy a used one for a fraction of the cost. Or we can take the bus, and save the money we would have spent on a car payment until we can afford to pay cash for a car.

Many things we think we need are really just wants. If we'll do without until we can pay cash, we'll avoid the stress and anxiety that comes with owing money. When we live within our means, instead of going into debt to live in a higher income bracket, we actually live more peaceful lives.

Dear Father, thank You for the sound financial advice You give in Your Word. Help me to live within my means. Amen.

FILLED WITH JOY

But let all who take refuge in you rejoice;
let them sing joyful praises forever. Spread
your protection over them, that all who
love your name may be filled with joy.

PSALM 5:11 NLT

Joy is often confused with happiness. While joy may be similar to happiness, the two concepts have entirely different sources. Happiness is based on what's happening right now. Joy is based on an assured, victorious future.

When we're in trouble, we can take refuge in God, and we can rejoice! We can—*and will*—sing His praises forever. All who love God, all who are called His children, will be filled with joy!

The reason for that joy is we know that, despite our present trouble, we have hope. We have the promise of a good future filled with love and peace, and absent from suffering and trials of every kind. Though we may not feel happy about our current circumstance, we can rejoice, because we know how our story will end.

Dear Father, I love You, and I take refuge in You.
Fill me with Your joy as I focus on the wonderful
future You have planned for me. Amen.

A RECKLESS FAITH

*By faith the people passed through the Red
Sea as on dry land; but when the Egyptians
tried to do so, they were drowned.*

HEBREWS 11:29 NIV

Sometimes God brings us to unexpected crossroads
in our faith. He longs for us to trust Him, so He
pushes us to the point of no return. We must either
rush into a towering wall of water and trust Him not
to let us drown; or we must run into the arms of the
enemy, who will certainly see to our demise. "Which
will it be?" God asks.

Nothing in the Israelites' past had prepared them
to walk through a deep sea without getting wet. For
all they knew, they'd die. Yet they knew it would be
better to drown while following God, than to die—or
even live—at the hands of the enemy.

So they rushed into the water, and God delivered
them more fully, more faithfully than they could
have imagined. Not only did they live, but their
enemies were destroyed because of that one act of
wild, reckless faith.

*Dear Father, teach me to have reckless
faith. I trust You. Amen.*

SAND ON THE FLAME

*In everything set them an example by doing what is
good. In your teaching show integrity, seriousness
and soundness of speech that cannot be condemned,
so that those who oppose you may be ashamed
because they have nothing bad to say about us.*

TITUS 2:7–8 NIV

Everywhere we go, we will encounter difficult people. It would be nice if God only created pleasant people, but God loves diversity. And part of celebrating people's differences is accepting that some people are going to be harder to get along with than others.

We can't stop difficult people from being, well, difficult. We can, however, give them as little as possible to be difficult about. This verse tells us that in everything we do, we need to set an example. Don't cut corners. Give more than is expected. Show kindness, generosity, and class. Don't gossip or slander. Show humility and treat others with respect.

When we live upright, blameless lives, we throw sand on a difficult person's flame. When we continuously show love and kindness, we make God proud, and He will bless us.

*Dear Father, help me to live a
blameless life. Amen.*

THINK ABOUT SUCH THINGS

Finally, brothers and sisters, whatever is true, whatever is noble, whatever is right, whatever is pure, whatever is lovely, whatever is admirable—if anything is excellent or praiseworthy—think about such things.

PHILIPPIANS 4:8 NIV

The type of fuel we put into our vehicles determines how well they run. If we use top-of-the-line gasoline, our cars operate more efficiently than if we use a cheap, watered-down version. The same is true for our minds. Our actions and emotions are often determined by our thoughts. When we feed ourselves positive, uplifting contemplations, those pure, noble thoughts turn into pure, noble feelings and actions.

If we struggle with depression, anger, fear, or other negative emotions, we should examine what we're feeding our brains. While some issues may require a doctor's care, we can certainly move our mental health in the right direction by controlling what we think about. We can push aside those damaging beliefs and replace them with God's Word and uplifting thoughts. When we do, we'll find everything in our lives takes on a more positive hue.

Dear Father, help me fill my mind with positive things. Amen.

LOVE ONE ANOTHER

*Owe nothing to anyone except to love one another;
for he who loves his neighbor has fulfilled the law.*

ROMANS 13:8 NASB

There are many things in life we can't control. While we may have limited power to change our circumstances, we can certainly do our best to live by God's standards. We shouldn't borrow money for something if we can do without it. But we should be ever mindful of the debt of love we owe to God. He wants us to pay that debt forward by loving other people.

When we love each other, that love comes back to us. It causes others to have good feelings about us, and they return the love. They help us when they can. It also pleases God, and He pours out His blessings on us. When we feel powerless to change our situations, we can look for ways to love other people. It may not solve all our problems, but it will certainly turn things around in the right direction.

*Dear Father, thank You for this reminder
to pay my debt of love forward. Show
me who needs love today. Amen.*

LOVING OURSELVES

For the whole law is fulfilled in one word:
"You shall love your neighbor as yourself."
But if you bite and devour one another, watch
out that you are not consumed by one another.

GALATIANS 5:14–15 ESV

Some of the most difficult people to be around are people who don't like themselves. Oh, it may seem like they love themselves and dislike everyone else, but that's not usually the case. When we don't like the person we see in the mirror each morning, we usually don't care much for anyone else either.

When we're commanded to love others as we love ourselves, it's a given that we actually love ourselves. God wants us to take care of our needs, show kindness to ourselves, and be gentle with our thoughts about ourselves. And He wants us to treat others that way as well.

When we love ourselves the way God loves us, and we love others in the same way—by taking care of their needs and showing kindness, gentleness, and respect—our relationships become healthy and fulfilling.

Dear Father, teach me to love myself,
so I can love others better. Amen.

THE HEALER

*"You shall serve the LORD your God, and he
will bless your bread and your water, and I
will take sickness away from among you."*

EXODUS 23:25 ESV

God warned the Israelites—and He warns us—against
the dangers of worshipping other gods. In a covenant contract with His people, He said, "If you do
this, I will do this." But if the Israelites chose to be
unfaithful, the covenant was void. Often, God in
His mercy chose to bless His people despite their
sin; but they couldn't expect the full benefits of His
promises if they weren't willing to keep up their end
of the bargain.

The same is true today. Disease exists because sin
exists in this world, and every one of us has sinned.
When we choose faithfulness to God as a lifestyle,
we may still be touched by disease. But that does
not negate His overwhelming love for us. When we
love Him with our whole hearts, we can cry out to
the healer, and He will bless us.

*Dear Father, You are the healer. Please
heal me, and heal those I love. Amen.*

DO NOT BE AFRAID

*When I saw Him, I fell at His feet like a
dead man. And He placed His right hand
on me, saying, "Do not be afraid; I am the
first and the last, and the living One."*

REVELATION 1:17–18 NASB

God is so awesome, so mighty and powerful, we can't help but feel afraid of Him. When we first stand in His presence, the essence of His greatness will overwhelm us. But this verse assures us, though we may tremble at the magnitude of His might, we have nothing to fear from Him.

God has existed in all His power since the beginning of time, and He will never cease to exist. Tied up in all that power is His overwhelming love for us, and He combines that love and power to work on our behalf through every season of our lives.

When circumstances leave us anxious about all kinds of things, we can pause, feel that gentle hand on our spirits, and hear His voice whisper, "Do not be afraid."

Dear Father, thank You for this reminder that You love me, and I don't need to be afraid. Amen.

HONOR YOUR PARENTS

Children, obey your parents in the Lord, for this is right. "Honor your father and mother" (this is the first commandment with a promise), "that it may go well with you and that you may live long in the land."

EPHESIANS 6:1–3 ESV

By design, parents love their children. Although there are exceptions, most parents want what is best for their offspring. Even the ungodly will teach good things to their children in hopes that they will succeed in life. When we listen to our parents' wisdom, we avoid making the same mistakes they made, and our lives are better.

This verse contains both a promise and a principle. When we listen to the people God has placed in authority over us as our parents—when we choose to honor them and make them proud—we choose a path of wisdom, which leads to triumphant living. And we can always find wisdom by seeking God's input, for He is the ultimate parent.

Dear Father, thank You for being the perfect parent. Help me to honor my earthly parents, and help me honor You. Amen.

NO NEED TO GRIEVE

*Now the LORD said to Samuel, "How long will you
grieve over Saul, since I have rejected him from
being king over Israel? Fill your horn with oil and
go; I will send you to Jesse the Bethlehemite, for I
have selected a king for Myself among his sons."*

1 SAMUEL 16:1 NASB

Elections can get pretty emotional. No matter where
we stand on the political spectrum, the issues that
are important to us seem crucial to our future health,
happiness, and well-being. When our candidate or
our cause doesn't win, we can feel devastated and
without hope.

But we need to remind ourselves that God has
it all under control. He knew the results of the current election before time began, and He's already
put everything in place to bring His perfect plan to
completion. There's no need to grieve the loss of an
election or an unfavorable turn of the political tide.
We just need to trust Him.

*Dear Father, please raise up a godly
leader. We need a David. Amen.*

WAIT FOR GOD

*I waited patiently for the LORD; he turned to me and
hear my cry. He lifted me out of the slimy pit, out
of the mud and mire; he set my feet on a rock and
gave me a firm place to stand. He put a new song in
my mouth, a hymn of praise to our God. Many will
see and fear the LORD and put their trust in him.*

PSALM 40:1–3 NIV

No one likes to wait. It's why many of us would
rather eat substandard food from a drive-through
than experience the joy of a home-cooked meal.
But many blessings can only be obtained through
patience and a lot of waiting.

Just look at the blessings David received because
he waited. First, God heard him. Then, God lifted him
out of the pit. Next, He set David on a rock and gave
him a firm place to stand. Finally, God put a song of
praise in David's heart.

Most of God's blessings are not of the fast-food
variety. Have patience, and wait for God. You'll be
glad you did.

*Dear Father, teach me to wait. I know You
have good things in store for me. Amen.*

OBEDIENCE—A SOUND DECISION

*By faith the walls of Jericho fell, after the army
had marched around them for seven days.*

HEBREWS 11:30 NIV

Armies are trained to fight. Yes, they march. Yes, they sometimes blow trumpets. But the real nitty-gritty of what an army is trained to do is advance, kill, destroy. When God asked the Israelites to march around the walls of Jericho and blow their trumpets, they must have felt a little ridiculous.

Faith can feel ridiculous at times. It defies logic. It doesn't make any sense. And yet the people of God know, from experience after experience, that faith actually makes perfect sense. No matter what God asks us to do—no matter how far-fetched it may seem—it is always the safest, soundest decision. For if God is for us, who can be against us (Romans 8:31)? When we obey God, we may feel ridiculous. But obedience is often followed by miracles. Trust Him. Obey Him. And watch those walls fall.

*Dear Father, I trust You. Help me obey You,
even when obedience feels strange. I believe
the walls in my life will fall. Amen.*

DOING GOOD

Let us not become weary in doing good,
for at the proper time we will reap a
harvest if we do not give up.

GALATIANS 6:9 NIV

Doing the right thing can be exhausting. Oh, we can all be good every once in a while. But making the right choices day after day—week after month after year—can wear us down, especially when the payoff awaits somewhere in the distant future.

Being *bad* is easier than doing *good*. Gossip can be addictive; it's hard to walk away or take a stand when we hear juicy secrets. Showing up late for work and leaving early is a lot easier than giving the extra half hour.

However, each time we make the difficult choice to do the right thing, we create a ripple effect that will eventually come back to us, bringing in a hefty harvest of God's peace and joy and goodwill. Small choice by small choice—with God's help—we can create an inheritance that, in the end, will be worth the sacrifice.

Dear Father, help me not to grow weary in doing
good. I want to honor You in all I do. Amen.

CHASING DREAMS

*Those who work their land will have abundant
food, but those who chase fantasies have no sense.*
PROVERBS 12:11 NIV

Hard work, more often than not, leads to our needs
being met. God wants us to chase our dreams—He
created those dreams, after all. But we must be sure
to balance those dreams with practical application.
We can pursue education and practice our skills to
get us where we want to be in life. In the meantime,
we sometimes have to do things we don't want to
do, in order to pay the bills.

Actors and actresses, chasing the dream, must
often wait tables in the process. Aspiring writers
must teach school; gifted musicians offer piano
lessons in ongoing, half-hour increments. When
we dedicate our dreams to God, He will find ways
for us to use our talents, even if we don't get paid
for it. But any honest job that brings a paycheck is
a blessing in itself, as our needs get met and we are
given the opportunity to bless others.

*Dear Father, help me balance my dreams
with practical application. Thank You
for giving me work. Amen.*

DELIVERED

Many are the afflictions of the righteous,
but the LORD delivers him out of them all.

PSALM 34:19 ESV

God's Word can be confusing. At times, He promises to protect the righteous from sickness and disease. At other times, He promises to deliver the righteous out of affliction. He can't deliver us out of something if we never experience it in the first place.

We live in a world where sin exists. Because sin broke the perfect system God created, we're all affected. Cancer, diabetes, arthritis, and even deadly flus are out there—and sometimes they settle in us. But for those who love God with their whole hearts, those afflictions don't get the final say! God will deliver us out of them all. Sometimes, that deliverance takes place here on earth. Other times, He delivers us straight out of this pain-filled existence into a pain-free, peace-filled, love-saturated eternity. Either way, we're delivered.

Dear Father, thank You for delivering me
from every affliction. I love You. I trust
You. I know You are good. Amen.

CARE FOR FAMILY

But if anyone does not provide for his own,
and especially for those of his household, he has
denied the faith and is worse than an unbeliever.

1 TIMOTHY 5:8 NASB

God created the family structure for our benefit. Parents take care of children when they are too young to care for themselves. Later, children should take care of their parents when they are too old or feeble to live on their own. This could mean physical care in the home, or it could mean financial assistance.

We are also to care for other family members. If those who have the means took care of their own families, we would eliminate some of the need for government assistance, and we'd give people dignity. As God's children, we are all part of the same spiritual family, and we should care for those around us. This can be a difficult task at times, but God will always bless those who honor Him in this way.

Dear Father, show me how I can care for
members of my family today. Amen.

GENTLE PARENTING

*Fathers, do not provoke your children to
anger, but bring them up in the discipline
and instruction of the Lord.*

EPHESIANS 6:4 ESV

Being a parent is hard. There's no way around it.
We pour our lives into our children, who are truly
individuals with their own personalities, gifts, and
talents. And those people—our children—make
their own choices. Sometimes, those choices don't
line up with what we've taught them or what we
want for them.

But God wants us to treat them with respect—the
same respect with which we'd treat a stranger. When
our children push and push us to the boiling point,
we're not supposed to retaliate in anger. When we speak
harshly and explode, we teach them to treat us the same
way, and it becomes an endless cycle. When we use
self-control and discipline them with love, kindness,
and respect, those lessons may not sink in immediately.
But we must have patience and persevere, knowing that
God will honor our efforts to act in love and gentleness,
even when we don't feel like it.

*Dear Father, help me not to provoke
my children to anger. Amen.*

PRAYER FOR HEALING

It happened that the father of Publius lay sick with fever and dysentery. And Paul visited him and prayed, and putting his hands on him, healed him.

ACTS 28:8 ESV

Miraculous healings took place in biblical times, and they still take place today. Prayer is a powerful tool—especially the prayer of a righteous man. So why doesn't God *always* choose to heal?

The answer is, we don't know. But it's helpful to remember that Paul spoke of his own affliction. While Paul prayed for others whom God chose to heal, Paul was never relieved of his own malady. Though it's hard to understand God's purpose sometimes, we do know that hardship makes us more compassionate. It draws us near to God. And it draws our focus to the eternal.

When we are sick, we should pray and ask for healing. We should also remember that God's ways are not our ways, and trust His love and purpose for our lives.

Dear Father, please heal me or my loved one. I trust You. Amen.

THE LIGHT

*"You, LORD, are my lamp; the LORD
turns my darkness into light."*

2 SAMUEL 22:29 NIV

Do you ever feel like the light has turned off inside
your soul? A depression is defined as a sunken place
or part, an area lower than the surrounding surface.
The psychological definition is a condition of general
emotional dejection and withdrawal, sadness
greater and more prolonged than that warranted by
any objective reason. It's a feeling of darkness, with
the unfounded belief that light is beyond our reach.

But God is our lamp! He does not run on electricity,
so His bulb will never burn out. When all is dark in our
spirits, we can reach for Him. He is right there. And the
more time we spend in His presence, the more we'll
see the glow of His light, illuminating the shadowy
places in our souls.

*Dear Father, thank You for being my light.
Everything feels dark right now, but I know
You are right here with me. Please drive away
my inner darkness, and drive away the gloom
with the brightness of Your love. Amen.*

FUTURE GENERATIONS

"When your days are complete and you lie down with your fathers, I will raise up your descendant after you, who will come forth from you, and I will establish his kingdom."

2 SAMUEL 7:12 NASB

Sometimes we worry about the political climate, not because of how it will affect us, but for our children's and grandchildren's sakes. But God, who has cared for us since before we drew our first breath, who has walked alongside each of our ancestors since before we have record of their existence, will not forsake our descendants. His faithfulness is unchanging, and His love never fails.

Not only will He take care of those who come after us, but He will raise up leaders of all kinds to bring about His perfect plan. While we should continue to pray, to vote, and to remain politically active as God calls us, we should not be anxious about the future. God will care for future generations, just as He has cared for us.

Dear Father, forgive me for worrying. I trust Your faithfulness and Your love. Amen.

ANXIOUS FOR NOTHING

Be anxious for nothing, but in everything by prayer and supplication with thanksgiving let your requests be made known to God. And the peace of God, which surpasses all comprehension, will guard your hearts and your minds in Christ Jesus.

PHILIPPIANS 4:6–7 NASB

Be anxious for *nothing*. The word *nothing* leaves no wiggle room. It's not okay, or even reasonable, for a follower of Christ to worry about *anything*. Though circumstances may overwhelm or frighten us, the only reasonable response for a Christian is to take those concerns directly to God in prayer and leave them with Him.

This verse takes prayer a step further. Supplication is humble prayer, entreaty, or petition. It's getting on our knees before God and pleading our case. Some might see a direct correlation between the level of humility and pleading in our prayers and the level of peace we walk away with. The more we empty our hearts and anxieties to God, the more He replaces them with good things.

Dear Father, thank You for this reminder to take everything to You in humble prayer and leave it with You. Amen.

GOD AND MAN

*"God is not man, that he should lie, or a son
of man, that he should change his mind.
Has he said, and will he not do it? Or has
he spoken, and will he not fulfill it?"*

NUMBERS 23:19 ESV

Sometimes our faith in mankind gets a little shaky.
And it should, because men are flawed. Even a good
person will let us down at times. When we base
our perception of God on our experiences with
other people, we will inevitably be disappointed.

But God is a far cry from any human! He cannot
lie. He cannot make mistakes. He cannot be anything
but good. Every breath we take, every step we take,
every moment of our lives, God is constantly working
for our good. If He promised it, we can be certain
He will deliver on that promise, no matter what.

*Dear Father, forgive me for ever doubting
You. I know You will keep all Your promises
to me. I trust You, and I know You are good.
Help me relax in that knowledge. Amen.*

A SOFT ANSWER

*A soft answer turns away wrath,
but a harsh word stirs up anger.*

PROVERBS 15:1 ESV

One thing that marks a difficult person is that he or she is easily angered. But even the most hot-tempered person's anger can be held at bay with kindness, gentleness, and respect. On the other hand, short, clipped answers, laced with impatience and sarcasm, will drive even a saint to resentment.

It takes self-control to keep our voices soft, our tones gentle. When someone annoys us, the last thing we want to do is show kindness. But the ounce of prevention that comes from a soft answer is well worth the pounds of bitterness and drama that a scathing response will bring.

When we find ourselves wanting, *needing* to respond in a harsh way, perhaps we should take a deep breath, toss up a prayer, and exercise some self-discipline. Instead of giving a biting retort, we can offer a pleasant surprise in the form of soothing words sprinkled with love.

*Dear Father, please help me develop self-control
in the way I speak to others. Help me show
love and kindness with my words. Amen.*

AN UNTROUBLED HEART

"Let not your heart be troubled;
you believe in God, believe also in Me."

JOHN 14:1 NKJV

This simply worded command is not as easy as it sounds. "Let not your heart be troubled." The implication is clear: our heart will want to be troubled. Circumstances will frustrate us; situations will lead us to anxiety and fear. Trouble is a preexisting condition of life.

Yet an act of our human will comes into play as well. "Let not your heart be troubled." That little word, *let*, implies that we have a choice. Our hearts will not remain in a troubled state without our permission. We only live in constant stress if we *allow* ourselves to live that way.

God stands ready, waiting, to take our troubles. He wants us to lay them down at His feet and go on with our lives, knowing He will take care of every detail.

Dear Father, thank You for this reminder that I do not have to be troubled. Help me lay the difficult things of my life at Your feet. Amen.

FOR PRACTICE

"So if you have not been trustworthy in handling worldly wealth, who will trust you with true riches?"

LUKE 16:11 NIV

The Bible tells us money is secondary to the true riches of heaven. Just as we give children play money to practice for when they will have real money, God wants us to view our cash as practice for the more intangible blessings He has in store for our lives. If we can handle our finances wisely, God will bless us with more. If we can't handle our money, why should God trust us with things that hold even more value?

When we view our finances as practice assignments to get us ready for more precious gifts, it eliminates some of the stress we put on ourselves. God will take care of us, but He also wants to see how well we can take care of what He's already given us.

Dear Father, help me to be wise with my money. Help me to be trustworthy with the things You've given me. Amen.

FORGIVENESS

Bear with each other and forgive one
another if any of you has a grievance against
someone. Forgive as the Lord forgave you.

COLOSSIANS 3:13 NIV

When people hurt us, forgiveness can feel like defeat. We often want to hang on to whatever grievances we have against others. We want to cuddle those bad memories in our laps as if they were a fluffy pet. We take them out, feed them, and caress them. We analyze them from every possible angle; and each time we do this, our anger grows bigger, until bitterness consumes us like a cancer.

Forgiveness isn't saying an action was okay. Instead, it's recognizing that the memory is a harmful one—harmful to ourselves and to our relationships with God and others—and making the choice to amputate it. When we forgive, we release the memory or event to God, to make room for good things in our own lives.

When someone hurts us, we should deal with it and get over it as quickly as we are able. Forgiveness frees us to live healthy, productive, love-filled lives.

Dear Father, help me forgive others the way
You've forgiven me—completely. Amen.

41

THE DELIVERER

For he will deliver the needy when he cries for help,
the afflicted also, and him who has no helper.

PSALM 72:12 NASB

Ideally, a government has the best interest of its people in mind with every decision made and every law passed. But governments are made up of people. People are flawed. People have limits. People mess up.

We should always pray for the people God has placed in positions of leadership. Yet we must never confuse our government with our source of help. We have a Deliverer. No matter what's going on with our taxes or our insurance or our laws, God is there. He hears our cries, and He already knows our needs. He has already set things into motion to rescue those who reach out to Him.

He loves us, and He—not our government—will deliver us. All we have to do is call.

> *Dear Father, please guide the leaders of*
> *our country and our world. Give them*
> *wisdom and compassion. You already know*
> *my needs. Please rescue me. Amen.*

GOD'S WHISPER

Your lovingkindness, O LORD, will hold me up.
When my anxious thoughts multiply within
me, Your consolations delight my soul.

PSALM 94:18–19 NASB

The psalmist didn't say, "*If* my anxious thoughts multiply within me." He used the word *when*. He knew those anxious thoughts would surely come, and they would certainly fill every space within us. Like fire ants, they will sting every part of our spirits. But he also knew we don't need to succumb to those fire-ant fears. God will hold us up and delight our souls.

Satan wants to destroy us from the inside out. He whispers our worst fears, filling our minds with anxiety. But Satan is a liar and a loser. We don't need to listen to him. When that voice of doubt fills our heads, we need to listen closer for God's whisper. He is there, reassuring us. He is there, holding us up. He is there, comforting us and filling our souls with delight.

Dear Father, thank You for Your loving-kindness,
which gives me strength. Thank You for delighting
my soul with Your love. Help me to hear
Your voice above all others. Amen.

FULLY SATISFIED

*A sluggard's appetite is never filled, but the
desires of the diligent are fully satisfied.*

PROVERBS 13:4 NIV

Have you ever noticed we often eat more when we're bored? That should come as no surprise, since the principle is recorded here in Proverbs. God designed us to work hard and be productive. When we have too much time on our hands, we get bored and fill our thoughts with all the things we wish we had—things we think will make us happy. It's an endless cycle, because we'll never have everything we wish for as long as we're on this earth. Our appetites will never be truly filled until we get to heaven.

But when we work hard, we don't have time to think about all the things we *don't* have. Our minds are filled with purpose and productivity. And when we rest from our work, we eat enough to satisfy us, and we sleep soundly. Even if the labor itself doesn't delight us, the effort we put into doing a job well gives us an immense feeling of fulfillment. Hard work leads to contentment and peace.

*Dear Father, help me find fulfillment
in hard work. Amen.*

A LIFE WELL LIVED

Who is wise and understanding among you?
By his good conduct let him show his works in the
meekness of wisdom. But if you have bitter jealousy
and selfish ambition in your hearts, do not boast
and be false to the truth. This is not the wisdom that
comes down from above, but is earthly, unspiritual,
demonic. For where jealousy and selfish ambition
exist, there will be disorder and every vile practice.

JAMES 3:13–16 ESV

When dealing with difficult people, it's easy to fall into the competition trap. We want to be better than the other person, and we want everyone to know we're better. But God's Word warns against this type of petty behavior. James encourages us to forget the competition and let our actions speak for themselves.

When we are good at something, people notice. When we are humble and kind, we don't have to exalt ourselves, because others will do it for us. When dealing with hard-to-handle people, it's often best to simply be what we know we should be—humble, kind, and hardworking.

Dear Father, help me to be more concerned with living right than with looking right. Amen.

HE WILL DELIVER

I sought the LORD, and He answered me,
and delivered me from all my fears.

PSALM 34:4 NASB

Sometimes we want God to deliver us just because we are His. We want Him to take care of our needs simply because He is our Father, and that's what fathers do. But we have a role to play in our deliverance as well. If we want answers, we must seek Him. If we want to be rescued from our anxieties, we must draw near to Him.

When we seek Him, He will respond. When we look for Him, He will save us. The answers don't come unless we ask. The rescue isn't promised unless we call out for help. When circumstances threaten to overwhelm us, we must ask ourselves, *Am I seeking God? Can I seek Him more?* When we draw as close to Him as we possibly can, He will be there. He will answer. He will deliver us from our fears.

> *Dear Father, I'm looking for You. I want to*
> *be as close to You as I can be. Amen.*

RADICAL HUMILITY

Do nothing out of selfish ambition or vain conceit.
Rather, in humility value others above yourselves.

<small>PHILIPPIANS 2:3 NIV</small>

Humility is perhaps the most radical, *unnatural* teaching we find in God's Word. It is in our nature—our *sinful* nature—to look out for number one. From birth, we cry when we're hungry and demand that someone feed us. We fuss when we want a diaper change or a toy. We expect our needs to be met by others. If we're not careful, that me-first attitude can stay with us throughout our lives, and it can consume us.

But God wants us to go against our selfish nature and put others before ourselves. He wants our joy to come from blessing others. Like the child who is more excited about *giving* a Christmas gift than *receiving* one, our loving, joyful humility is a blessing to others and a delight to God.

Dear Father, please teach me to exercise radical, joyful humility. Help me find immense satisfaction in putting others before myself. Amen.

GO BOLDLY

*Let us then with confidence draw near to the
throne of grace, that we may receive mercy
and find grace to help in time of need.*

HEBREWS 4:16 ESV

Not just anyone is allowed to barge in on a king or queen. But the royal children—the sons and daughters of the Royal Highness—are allowed, even invited, to approach the throne with boldness. That's us! We are sons and daughters of the King. We are cherished and adored. When we want or need something, God wants us to talk to Him. He'll always meet our needs, and He will often grant our wants as well.

When it comes to our physical health, God longs for us to come to Him. He created us for a relationship with Him. Though He doesn't cause bad things to happen to us, He sometimes allows them in order to draw us near. Go boldly to Him today. Tell Him what's on your mind, and listen to His response. We are always blessed by spending time in His presence.

*Dear Father, I love You with all my heart.
Please have mercy on me. Please heal
me, and heal those I love. Amen.*

WISE INHERITANCE

A good person leaves an inheritance for
their children's children, but a sinner's
wealth is stored up for the righteous.

PROVERBS 13:22 NIV

In the New Testament, Timothy tells us that the love of money is the root of all kinds of evil. This promise from Proverbs shows a different side of that statement. Good people love other people more than they love money. They love their children and grandchildren so much, they set aside money as an inheritance instead of spending all their money on themselves.

The love of money can affect anyone, whether rich or poor. The poor can love money so much they'll do anything to get it. The rich can love money so much that they never feel they have enough. But love of money is an addiction that will never satisfy our spirit's deepest longing. Only love for God and other people will fill the deep hunger in our souls. The wise person sets aside money to leave behind, as an act of love and sacrifice.

Dear Father, teach me to love other people
more than I love money. Amen.

TRUST HIM TO ACT

Commit your way to the LORD;
trust in him, and he will act.

PSALM 37:5 NRSV

Trusting God can be hard. After all, what if He doesn't do what we want Him to do? What if things don't turn out the way we planned? Too often, it's easy to take our troubles to God, show Him what they look like, and then walk away with those issues still in our grasp. When we do that, we haven't really committed anything to Him. We haven't trusted Him.

God is a gentleman, and He will not force our problems out of our tightfisted grip. Either we want Him to take care of things, or we'll take care of them ourselves. We can't have it both ways.

If we want to see God move, we must trust Him. When we loosen our grip and leave our trials in God's capable hands, that's when He will act.

Dear Father, trust is hard for me. I know You can
handle my problems much better than I can. I
give them to You now, and I trust You. Amen.

UNFAILING LOVE

Many are the woes of the wicked, but the LORD's
unfailing love surrounds the one who trusts in him.
PSALM 32:10 NIV

This verse tells us the wicked will have many woes.
Yet most of us don't like to think of ourselves as
wicked! Why then does it feel like sorrow surrounds
us on every side?

We know that God doesn't necessarily remove
all our sorrows. Sadness and hardship are a part
of life. But when we stay close to our Lord, when
we trust His goodness through every difficulty, we
feel His presence. His love surrounds us. It gives
us strength and courage and joy and a peace that
surpasses understanding.

When we trudge through life without trusting
in God, those sorrows will indeed overtake us. But
when we trust Him, His love lifts us up.

Dear Father, sometimes I feel overwhelmed with
sorrow. I trust in Your goodness and Your love.
Surround me with Your presence, Lord, and carry
me through this difficult time. I love You. Amen.

ALL THINGS

I can do all this through him who gives me strength.
PHILIPPIANS 4:13 NIV

It's a wonderful feeling when we know we're capable of conquering whatever task lies before us. But sometimes we're given a task that seems beyond us—beyond our abilities. At those times, we may do our best, and our best may not seem good enough. During those times, it can feel like a spotlight is being shined on our weakest, most unattractive qualities.

Believe it or not, God loves it when we find ourselves out of our league! If we're capable of doing a job, we get the credit when it's completed. But if a task goes beyond our abilities, and we call on God to help us accomplish it, He gets the glory! He lives to give love and to receive glory. When we find ourselves in an impossible situation, we can smile, knowing He will show up whenever we call.

Dear Father, thank You for the reminder that I can do all things, not through my own strength, but through Christ, who strengthens me. Amen.

THE HIGH ROAD

*If possible, so far as it depends
on you, live peaceably with all.*

ROMANS 12:18 ESV

This verse contains such a lofty standard. We read it, and we can't help but nod in agreement. After all, who doesn't want world peace?

The execution of this verse is more difficult, especially when we're dealing with impossible people. After all, some people won't be pleased no matter what. Some people just aren't happy unless they're miserable. How are we supposed to change them?

We can't control anyone else. But we can control our own words and actions. Paul didn't say we must live at peace with everyone—he knew that some people are impossible to please. But he encourages us to do everything we can—within God's standards and good ethics—to live at peace with others. It may be difficult at times, but it is always right to take the high road, be the bigger person, and show love in the face of adversity.

*Dear Father, help me to do everything within
my power to live at peace with others. Amen.*

53

A LIFE OF FAITH

*By faith Noah, being warned by God concerning
events as yet unseen, in reverent fear constructed
an ark for the saving of his household. By this
he condemned the world and became an heir
of the righteousness that comes by faith.*

Faith in God sometimes requires us to stand against
the world. Others will laugh at us and call us fools.
They will say we're old-fashioned, or that we're
missing out. They'll encourage us to do what *feels*
right, instead of what *is* right.

A life of faith requires foresight. It requires a belief
in God's goodness that's even stronger than the belief
in the here and now. Noah knew God loved him and
that God must have had His reasons for telling him
to build an ark. He trusted God, and he obeyed.
Because his faith was backed up with obedience,
even when others called him a fool, Noah and his
family were saved.

> *Dear Father, I trust You, and I believe in
> Your goodness. Help me to act in faith, even
> when others don't understand. Amen.*

WANTS AND NEEDS

*Wise people's houses are full of the best foods and
olive oil, but fools waste everything they have.*

PROVERBS 21:20 NCV

Foolish people look forward to payday so they can
spend that money on whatever they want. A week
after payday, they have nothing to show for their
hard work. These people always seem to have a
good time, but they never have money set aside for
emergencies or larger purchases.

One of the hardest lessons to learn is the difference between our wants and our needs. When we
learn to do without many of our wants, we often
find we have more than enough to meet our needs.
When we save our money, we eventually find we
can face emergencies or make large purchases with
ease. The wise person has learned to save money
for occasional luxurious purchases and for unexpected disasters instead of spending every dime on
immediate pleasures.

*Dear Father, help me to be wise with my money.
Teach me the difference between my wants and
my needs, and help me develop self-discipline to
save money instead of spending it all. Amen.*

WORDS OF BLESSING

*Do not let any unwholesome talk come out
of your mouths, but only what is helpful for
building others up according to their needs,
that it may benefit those who listen.*

EPHESIANS 4:29 NIV

A few synonyms for *unwholesome* are *unpleasant*,
distasteful, and *harmful*. The Bible warns against
unwholesome talk, but our society seems to encourage it. Whether it's foul language, gossip, or
lewd discussions, unwholesome talk is everywhere.

Negative talk will never bring about the pleasant,
peace-filled lives we long for. When we use foul language, we set a mood that follows us like a dark cloud.
When we gossip, we send the message that we can't
be trusted, for those who gossip about one person will
usually gossip about any person. When we participate in
lewd conversations, we disrespect ourselves and others.

God wants our words to be positive and encouraging. He wants blessings, not curses, to flow from
our mouths. When we make affirming, uplifting
words a way of life, others are drawn to us, and we
find more joy and peace in our relationships.

*Dear Father, help me guard my tongue and only
speak pleasant, uplifting words. Amen.*

A CALL TO ACTION

Humble yourselves, therefore, under God's mighty hand, that he may lift you up in due time. Cast all your anxiety on him because he cares for you.

1 PETER 5:6–7 NIV

When we feel depressed, we want to curl up in a ball and let life do what it will. But overcoming depression requires battle. It calls for action on our parts.

First, we must humble ourselves. We must recognize that although things may not be exactly as we want them to be, it's not the end of the world. One day, God will reward our faithfulness and lift us up. Being humble requires a decision on our parts to accept that life isn't perfect, God doesn't follow our timeline, and it's okay.

Next we must cast our anxieties on Him. Casting isn't the same as dropping or laying. Casting means using all our strength and actually hefting our cares in His direction. When we fling our worries and concerns toward the Almighty, He will catch them. He will remove them from our shoulders and carry them.

Dear Father, with all my strength, I throw my cares to You. Thank You for taking them from me. Amen.

OVERCOMER

*For everyone who has been born of God
overcomes the world. And this is the victory
that has overcome the world—our faith.*

1 JOHN 5:4 ESV

Most coaches want to be in charge of the winning team. Satan is no different—he wants to win. But while most coaches want each of their players to *feel* like winners, Satan is the opposite. Satan wants the people under his power to feel like losers. He wants us to be discouraged and defeated.

God, on the other hand, wants each and every one of His children to be winners. He wants us to be overcomers in this life. He knows we're competing both as a team and as individuals, and He longs for each of us to walk through each day as victors. He's given us everything we need to be successful in every way that's important—and the main ingredient to that success is our faith. When we trust Him—believing with everything in us that we're on the winning team—we become overcomers.

*Dear Father, thank You for making
me an overcomer. My faith is in You
and no one else. Amen.*

INHERITANCE FROM THE LORD

*You know that you will receive an
inheritance from the Lord as a reward.
It is the Lord Christ you are serving.*

COLOSSIANS 3:24 NIV

It's difficult to work for a boss who doesn't appreciate us. Basic human appreciation is, in some ways, even more important than a paycheck. When we work hard and do our best and no one seems to notice, it can drag down our spirits and make us want to give up.

But we serve a Master who adores us! We must never forget—no matter what humans may say or do—God sees, and He appreciates our hard work. It is Him we serve, and He has a great reward, an impressive inheritance, waiting for us. When we feel undervalued and taken advantage of, we must remember for whom we're really working. He sees, He knows, and He cares.

Dear Father, thank You for the inheritance You've promised me. You know it's unpleasant to feel unappreciated. Please place people around me who will appreciate my contributions. Amen.

PRAYER OF FAITH

*And the prayer of faith will save the one who
is sick, and the Lord will raise him up. And if he
has committed sins, he will be forgiven. Therefore,
confess your sins to one another and pray for one
another, that you may be healed. The prayer of a
righteous person has great power as it is working.*

JAMES 5:15–16 ESV

God wants our focus to be on our spiritual health,
even more than our physical health. That's hard to do
when we're in pain, or when we face the possibility
of great loss. But as difficult as it is to see, the truth
is that sin does far greater damage to our lives than
any physical ailment.

God wants us to confess our sins and turn away
from them. He wants us to trust Him with our physical
needs. When we do these things, God saves
us. He heals our spirits. And often, He will heal us
physically as well.

*Dear Father, I know I am sinful. Please forgive me
of my sins and help me to turn away from anything
that offends You. I trust You with my life. Amen.*

LASTING PEACE

"Peace I leave with you; my peace I give to you. I do not give to you as the world gives. Do not let your hearts be troubled, and do not let them be afraid."

JOHN 14:27 NRSV

This world has some pretty impressive gifts to offer. With enough money, we can purchase just about anything. . .even peace. Or at least, a glittery, high-dollar version of peace in the form of a seven-day cruise or an all inclusive spa resort vacation. But that kind of peace is temporary. We always have to return to the real world and its real troubles.

God gives the kind of peace that lasts and lasts. We can take it anywhere, access it anytime. We don't have to dream about it like some elusive, distant-future vacation package. It's right here, right now. And the best part about it? God's gift of peace is free. All we have to do is trust Him.

Dear Father, thank You for Your gift of peace. Remind me that Your peace is there, free for the taking, anytime I choose to accept it. Amen.

BEHAVING BADLY

Whoever brings trouble to his family
will be left with nothing but the wind.
A fool will be a servant to the wise.

PROVERBS 11:29 NCV

Bad behavior is disrespectful to the people around us—particularly the people in our families who have to deal with the consequences of our actions. When we make choices that damage our reputations and diminish our ability to carry a good name in our community, we harm our families. We embarrass them. We bring shame on them. When we behave badly, we mess up our important relationships, often for a really long time.

When families live in harmony with one another, good things occur. Relationships are healthy and strong, and love abounds. We must remember, wherever we are and whatever we do, our actions affect those who love us most. When we choose to live righteous, upright lives, we bring honor and blessing to our families, our relationships, and ourselves.

Dear Father, forgive me for bad decisions I've made
that have affected the people I love the most. Help me
to honor them—and You—with my choices. Amen.

PAYING OUT KINDNESS

*"So whatever you wish that others would do to you,
do also to them, for this is the Law and the Prophets."*
MATTHEW 7:12 ESV

Our culture seems to encourage an entitlement attitude. Too often, we feel others owe us something, but we don't think we owe them anything. But Christ encourages us to think of what we want for ourselves, and then do that for others. This is contrary to our nature, but it leads to a much more contented and fulfilling life.

When we find ourselves frustrated because others don't treat us the way we want to be treated, we should challenge ourselves to make a game of it. How can we treat the other person the way we'd want to be treated? Often, this type of giving attitude causes others to soften toward us and brings about the kind actions we desire for ourselves. Even if that doesn't happen, we will experience much more peace and joy in our lives by paying out kindness to others.

Dear Father, help me treat others the way I want them to treat me, even when it's hard. Amen.

WHEN HE'S READY

There will be no end to the increase of His
government or of peace, on the throne of
David and over his kingdom, to establish it
and to uphold it with justice and righteousness
from then on and forevermore. The zeal of
the LORD of hosts will accomplish this.

ISAIAH 9:7 NASB

When we read this promise, made so long ago by
God through the prophet Isaiah, we feel both excited
and dismayed. *How long?* may be the first question
that enters our minds. *When, Lord? When will this*
government of peace come? When will You reign here,
as You do in heaven?

The answer to that is simple. He will come when
He is ready, and He's not ready yet. In the meantime, we wait. We prepare our hearts. And we do
His work, which is sharing the message of His love
with everyone we meet. One day, when the time is
right, He will come.

Dear Father, please hurry. We need You. In the
meantime, keep me busy working for You. Amen.

SUFFICIENT GRACE

*And He has said to me, "My grace is sufficient
for you, for power is perfected in weakness."
Most gladly, therefore, I will rather boast about
my weaknesses, so that the power of Christ
may dwell in me. Therefore I am well content
with weaknesses, with insults, with distresses,
with persecutions, with difficulties, for Christ's
sake; for when I am weak, then I am strong.*
2 Corinthians 12:9–10 nasb

Anxiety is considered, by most, to be a weakness. But if we are weak, praise God! That weakness simply provides an opportunity for God to act on our behalf. When we go to our Father and admit our weakness, when we hand our anxiety to Him—He takes over. He fills us with His strength, and He acts in our best interest.

We don't have to be strong enough. He is more than capable of handling any problem, any fear we face. When we're afraid, we can let go of those fears, take a deep breath, and watch Him act.

*Dear Father, I know when I'm weak, You
show off Your power. Thank You for
taking over my fears. Amen.*

NEVER FORGOTTEN

"For I will restore health to you, and your wounds I will heal, declares the LORD, because they have called you an outcast: 'It is Zion, for whom no one cares!'"

JEREMIAH 30:17 ESV

It's so easy to forget about the sick among us. Most of us have good intentions, but life gets in the way; and before we know it, our good intentions have fallen short. Sometimes, when we're sick and we feel forgotten, it can feel like God has forgotten us.

But unlike humans, who are flawed and forgetful, God *always* sees. He *always* knows. He will never forget us. Not only does He remember us with great interest, but His compassion is unending. He says, "I will restore health to you," meaning He will give you good things. He also promises, "Your wounds I will heal," meaning He will take away the bad things. When life is lonely and hard, and our health leaves us feeling like an outcast, we must remember God cares deeply for His children. He has not forgotten us.

Dear Father, please restore my health and let me feel Your presence. Amen.

KEEP BREATHING

Anyone who is among the living has hope.

ECCLESIASTES 9:4 NIV

Hope is such a beautiful word. It is the assurance of good things to come. The author of Ecclesiastes wanted to make sure we know the importance of that word. As long as we're still breathing, we can know good things await us.

God calls Himself a God of hope. When we make Him our God and stay close to Him, there is no end to the goodness we'll receive. He loves us, and He wants to pour out His blessings on those who cling to Him. Even when things seem dark, we can know, without doubt, that light is surely just around the next bend. Every step we take leads us closer to the beautiful fulfillment of God's promises of peace and joy, mercy and grace.

No matter how hard life may seem at the moment, keep breathing. Each time you fill your lungs with oxygen, you can fill your spirit with the knowledge that good things are on the way.

*Dear Father, thank You for the promise
of good things to come. Help me
understand that hope. Amen.*

THE GOOD JUDGE

"In a certain city there was a judge who neither
feared God nor respected man. And there
was a widow in that city who kept coming to
him and saying, 'Give me justice against my
adversary.' For a while he refused, but afterward
he said to himself, 'Though I neither fear God
nor respect man, yet because this widow keeps
bothering me, I will give her justice.'"

LUKE 18:2–5 ESV

What a great story, and a great reminder of what persistent, faith-filled prayers can do. Truly, if an ungodly judge will deliver a good verdict just to shut someone up, how much more will our all-loving, all-compassionate, all-merciful Father take care of the injustice in our lives?

God wants our faith. He wants us to trust in His goodness and believe in His loving-kindness. When we pray, believing He will deliver exactly what we need, He will not turn His face away. He will answer every time.

Dear Father, thank You for seeing the injustice in my
life. I trust You to take care of my every need. Amen.

ON GIVING

*"Give, and you will receive. You will be given much.
Pressed down, shaken together, and running
over, it will spill into your lap. The way you give
to others is the way God will give to you."*

LUKE 6:38 NCV

The biblical principle of giving applies to more than just money. When we have a deficit in our lives, we can often trace it to a deficit in our own giving. If we're struggling in a relationship, instead of blaming the other guy, we can examine our own actions. Is there a way we can give more to the relationship? Can we be more loving and kind? How can we put the other person's needs ahead of our own?

If we're struggling in a job, we can ask ourselves if we're giving the time and commitment that is required, or are we giving the minimum we can give to draw a paycheck? When we give generously, whether we're giving money or time or compassion, our gifts have a way of multiplying and coming back to us.

*Dear Father, teach me to be a
generous giver like You. Amen.*

DILIGENCE

Diligent hands will rule, but
laziness ends in forced labor.
PROVERBS 12:24 NIV

According to a dictionary of modern terms, the phrase "like a boss" means to do something as a boss would do it. It refers to someone who takes charge and shows extreme competence in an area. God wants us to do our work "like a boss." When we work hard, with diligence and competence, people notice, and we will often get promoted in our jobs. According to this scripture, when we commit ourselves to a job well done, we very well may end up ruling, or being the boss.

But when we cut corners—when we show up late and leave early, when we take longer breaks than we're allowed—we bring trouble on ourselves. We often end up having to work harder, for less pay, than if we simply provided our best effort from the beginning. Laziness never brings about the happiness and fulfillment we all desire.

Dear Father, teach me to work hard and to
be diligent. I want to please You, and I want
to be successful in my job. Amen.

NEVER ALONE

It is better to take refuge in the
LORD than to trust in man.
PSALM 118:8 NASB

Friends are a blessing and a gift from God. If we find
a friend we can truly trust, we are doubly blessed.
But even the most sincere, loyal, trustworthy friend
will let us down sometimes. We are all human, and
sooner or later, we're all going to fail.

In God, we have a friend like no other. He will
never leave us, forsake us, or fail us. We can pour out
our deepest, most shameful secrets to Him and know
He will never use that information against us. He
loves us with perfect love and unfailing compassion.

When we feel alone, we can ask God to send us
earthly friends. But we can also know that, no matter
how alone we may feel, we don't have to be lonely.
We have a friend, and we can trust Him.

Dear Father, thank You for reminding me that I
can always trust You, and I'm never alone. Amen.

WHO YOU ARE

*"I say to you, do not be worried about your life,
as to what you will eat or what you will drink;
nor for your body, as to what you will put on.
Is not life more than food, and the body more
than clothing? Look at the birds of the air, that
they do not sow, nor reap nor gather into barns,
and yet your heavenly Father feeds them. Are
you not worth much more than they?"*

MATTHEW 6:25–26 NASB

God must shake His head at our anxieties and ask Himself, "When will they learn?" He takes such loving care of us, and yet we continue to worry about things. Though we may not always get everything we want, God will always make sure His children have what we need to get through this life and to become more like Him.

He takes care of all His creation, from birds to fish to plants. But we are more than just His creation. We are His children! When we feel anxious, we can remind ourselves who we are and how much He loves us.

Dear Father, thank You for taking care of me. Amen.

THE GOOD FIGHT

*Fight the good fight of faith, grabbing hold
of the life that continues forever. You were
called to have that life when you confessed the
good confession before many witnesses.*

1 TIMOTHY 6:12 NCV

The only thing we should fight, within our families or elsewhere, is the good fight of faith. We should press on, fighting against sin and evil and darkness, fighting for what is good and holy and right. We should fight for love, peace, purity, kindness, and compassion.

Satan wants to divert our attention from the good fight by getting us all up in arms about petty disagreements. When we fight over what we'll eat for dinner, which television show we'll watch, or who-said-what-with-that-tone-of-voice, we lose focus of what is important. We need to be aware of these minor distractions. When we respond to conflict with gentleness, kindness, and love, we make great advances for the good fight of faith, which leads to a victorious life.

Dear Father, help me fight the good fight. Keep me from getting distracted by petty conflicts. Amen.

WITHOUT JUDGMENT

"Judge not, that you be not judged."

MATTHEW 7:1 ESV

Time and again in God's Word, we are warned against judging others. God is the only one with that privilege. After all, God is the only one who truly knows a person's heart. He is the only one who knows the extent of a person's circumstances.

When we judge another person, we only see part of the story. We don't know what led a person to the place they are now. We don't know what deep hurts they may carry, or their level of desperation that may lead them to act inappropriately.

God is clear in His Word about His job and our jobs. Our job is to love others. Period. His job is to judge. When we judge others, we take on God's job. If we want God to show mercy and compassion when He judges us, we must not try to take His job from Him. We're much better off when we stick to doing our own job well: loving others without judgment.

Dear Father, forgive me for judging others and trying to do Your job. Help me to love, not judge. Amen.

VICTORIOUS!

"I have told you these things, so that in me you may have peace. In this world you will have trouble. But take heart! I have overcome the world."

JOHN 16:33 NIV

Hardship is a fact of life. God gave us free choice. Because He's not a dictator, He doesn't force us to act the way He wants us to act. Free choice means that some will make poor choices, and those poor choices cause sin. Sin affects us, and it affects those around us. Because of sin, every single person has to deal with trouble.

But we can have peace as we deal with each of our difficulties! When we rely on Christ alone for our strength, we can know we're on the winning team. The battle may be a rough one, but He has already won. We can relax in the knowledge that He has already defeated every hardship we face. We are winners. We are victors. We are overcomers.

Dear Father, thank You for Christ. Thank You that in You, I can be an overcomer. Amen.

THE GOD OF HOPE

May the God of hope fill you with all joy and
peace in believing, so that by the power of
the Holy Spirit you may abound in hope.

ROMANS 15:13 ESV

We often need to be reminded of the definition of hope. It is the belief that good things will come, no matter what. Hope is the opposite of fear, which is the belief that bad things will come.

God is the God of hope. He is only good; and when we stay close to Him, that goodness spills into our lives. Though not everything feels good in the moment, God's presence in our lives will fill us with joy and peace and hope. Our faith is simply the unwavering belief in God's goodness. When we feel our faith waning, we can remind ourselves of how God has shown His character to us—and to others before us, throughout time. God's love for us never changes. In Him, we can have confident hope.

Dear Father, thank You for Your steadfast goodness.
Please fill me with joy, peace, and hope. Amen.

TIME, TALENT, TREASURE

Honor the LORD with your wealth and the firstfruits
from all your crops. Then your barns will be full,
and your wine barrels will overflow with new wine.
PROVERBS 3:9–10 NCV

This verse isn't a promise of riches. Instead, it's a principle. The book of Proverbs is filled with good principles for every aspect of our lives. When we put God first in our lives—when we honor Him with our best instead of giving Him what's left over—He takes care of us. When we give to God the first of our time, our talent, and our treasure, we tend to look at everything we have differently.

Giving to God feels good. It changes something within us and creates a subtle shift in our values. We realize that going out to eat or buying that five-dollar coffee every day doesn't give us the fulfillment that generosity does. Giving to God may not put us on the Fortune 500 list, but it will give us something far better: a closeness with God that cannot be matched.

Dear Father, teach me to be generous. Amen.

EARNING A PROFIT

All hard work brings a profit, but
mere talk leads only to poverty.

PROVERBS 14:23 NIV

There's a saying, "You have to spend money to make money." Some of us don't have money to spend in the first place; but we all have something that's even more valuable than money: *time.* We have the ability to work hard for what we want. When we put in the time with hard work and diligence, we will see a profit.

Too often, we want to sit around and talk about the fact that we don't have money to spend, or what we'd do if we had the money. We dream about what we "might" do one day, if given the opportunity. The author of this proverb encourages us to stop talking! If there's something we want to do, we should do it. We should work hard at it. Talk is cheap; only time and hard work will lead to success.

Dear Father, help me to stop talking and dreaming,
and to get busy actually doing! I'm willing to
work hard to make my dreams come true, and I
trust You with all the things I can't do. Amen.

JOY IN EVERY MOMENT

But the Pharisees went out and conspired
against him, how to destroy him. Jesus, aware
of this, withdrew from there. And many
followed him, and he healed them all.

MATTHEW 12:14–15 ESV

Jesus was going through one of the most difficult times of His life. His circumstances were unfair. He'd spent His life loving God and serving others, and now the Pharisees conspired to kill Him. When faced with this knowledge, He withdrew to spend time with God, and He poured Himself out for others.

When an illness conspires to destroy us and threatens to take our lives, we can respond as Jesus did. Withdraw to God and serve others. When we fall into God, our heavenly Father will embrace us—consume us, even—with a love that surpasses understanding. When we pour our lives into serving others—even to our last breath—we forget about ourselves, our hardships, and our pain, and we find joy in every moment.

Dear Father, I love You. I want to pour myself
into You and into others. Show me how. Amen.

THE SEVENTH DAY

*Then God blessed the seventh day and made
it holy, because on it he rested from all the
work of creating that he had done.*

GENESIS 2:3 NIV

We all like to rest. We often spend our workweek dreaming and scheming and planning what we'll do on our day off; and when that day comes, it's a glorious thing. But this verse isn't only about the day of rest. It's about what happens on the other six days—hard work.

When we don't work hard, our rest isn't as fulfilling. When we don't work hard, the reward seems shallow. God rested because He was *finished*. He was *fulfilled*. He was *satisfied* with a job well done. Since we are made in His image, He wants us to know the same satisfaction and fulfillment that comes from being bone weary after a successful, diligent workweek.

When we labor with our full energy and commitment, God blesses our efforts. He gives us rest; and that kind of rest brings contentment, gratification, and true pleasure.

*Dear Father, teach me what it means
to work hard. Amen.*

GIVING OUR BEST

"Every man shall give as he is able,
according to the blessing of the LORD
your God which He has given you."

DEUTERONOMY 16:17 NKJV

God doesn't need our money. He created the world and controls it all! What He longs for, what He desires most, is our hearts. When we give our leftovers to God, He feels hurt—the same way we would feel wounded if our spouse forgot our birthday and only brought us a hurriedly bought card from the corner store. If that card were carefully chosen, and the spouse sacrificed to get it, we'd feel loved. If it were an afterthought, we'd feel slighted.

When we give our first and our best to God, we're sending Him a message that we love Him—that He is the most important thing in our lives, and that we're grateful for His presence. The size of the gift doesn't matter nearly as much as the sentiment behind it.

Dear Father, I want to give You as much
as I am able. Teach me to give You my
best, not my leftovers. Amen.

TRUSTWORTHY POWER

"I form light and create darkness; I make well-being and create calamity; I am the LORD, who does all these things."

ISAIAH 45:7 ESV

It's often so easy to focus on God's goodness that we forget His power. But it is God's power that will deliver us from every bad thing in our lives. It is His power that will carry us through the waves and see us through the storms. It is His power that will rescue us from each and every calamity.

Sometimes, God stirs things up in our lives just to see if we'll run to Him or away from Him. Just as any good teacher will test a student to see where he or she stands, God offers up tests of our faith. He wants to see if we've learned to trust Him or not.

The correct answer, no matter our circumstance, is to trust God. Trust His goodness. Trust His power. And know that He will always bring good from evil for those who cling to Him.

Dear Father, thank You for Your power. I trust You. Amen.

GOD'S PROTECTION

*"Every word of God is flawless; he is a
shield to those who take refuge in him."*

PROVERBS 30:5 NIV

A shield is a piece of armor meant for defense. When a warrior has his shield in place, it protects him from wounds of the enemy. But a shield is heavy, cumbersome, and hard to carry. If a soldier drops his shield, he puts himself in danger of being seriously injured or killed. No matter how tired the soldier may become, it's imperative that he keep his shield firmly in place.

Trusting God is the key to receiving His protection. We all want God to keep us safe and happy, but trust can be difficult. When we fail to trust God, we drop our shields and put ourselves in peril. If we want God's protection from the enemy's wounds, we must remain strong in our resolve to trust God.

*Dear Father, trust—like a shield—can be
heavy and difficult. Sometimes it's tempting
to trust myself or something else, but I know
that's like dropping my shield. Help me to
trust You, even when it's hard. Amen.*

COMPASSION

When he went ashore he saw a great crowd, and
he had compassion on them and healed their sick.

MATTHEW 14:14 ESV

Everywhere Jesus went, crowds followed Him. He just wanted a little time to Himself, time alone with His Father. But when He returned from His retreat, the crowds were still there, waiting, desperate. Everybody wanted a piece of Him.

But instead of getting frustrated, Jesus felt compassion for them. He healed their sick, because He knew He was the only one who could. In the same way, He feels compassion for us. When we are sick, when we are desperate, His heart is stirred, and He is moved to reach out to us.

When it seems Jesus has disappeared, just wait. Be patient. You will once again feel His presence in your life; and when you do, He will pour out His love, mercy, compassion, and healing.

Dear Father, at times, it feels like You've
disappeared. Help me to wait patiently for
You, Father. I am desperate for Your presence,
Your power, and Your healing. Amen.

ALL-POWERFUL GOD

*"By me kings reign and rulers issue decrees
that are just; by me princes govern, and
nobles—all who rule on earth."*

PROVERBS 8:15–16 NIV

It's easy to feel discouraged, or even devastated, when someone rises to political power that we feel is not suited for the job. Yet God's Word is filled with stories of God using the bad guys to bring about His purpose.

Look at Xerxes. He wasn't necessarily a bad guy, but he certainly wasn't a believer. But God used him, and his love for a pretty face (Esther) to save the Israelites. He used Jeroboam II, one of the most evil kings in scripture, to save His people. He used Joseph's jealous brothers to catapult Joseph into a position where he'd eventually rise to power and, yes, save God's people.

God is all-powerful, and He is only good. He is able to use evil people without being contaminated by that evil. No matter who is in power, we can trust God. He's got it all under control.

*Dear Father, thank You for this reminder
that You are in control. Amen.*

POWERFUL STUFF

For I am convinced that neither death nor life, neither angels nor demons, neither the present nor the future, nor any powers, neither height nor depth, nor anything else in all creation, will be able to separate us from the love of God that is in Christ Jesus our Lord.

ROMANS 8:38–39 NIV

The author of Romans certainly had a poetic style. He paints such a powerful, visual picture of the all-consuming nature of God's love for each of us. There is nothing—*absolutely nothing!*—that can separate us from the love of God in Christ Jesus.

That includes difficulties we may encounter. God's love is right there! That includes sins we commit and mistakes we make. God's love won't budge an inch! No matter what situation we may find ourselves in, we can know God's love is with us. It surrounds us on all sides. When we accept Christ as our Savior, the deal is sealed. He will never, ever remove His love from us.

That's pretty powerful stuff.

Dear Father, thank You for Your love that will never leave me, no matter what. Amen.

DIFFICULT PEOPLE

The vexation of a fool is known at once,
but the prudent ignores an insult.

PROVERBS 12:16 ESV

When it comes to dealing with difficult people, one of the wisest things we can do is play dumb. Or, as the writer of this verse says, we can ignore an insult—pretend we didn't even hear it or that we don't understand its intent.

Difficult people thrive on conflict. If their efforts at vexing us go unnoticed, they'll become frustrated and move on. But if they know they've pushed our buttons, they'll feel successful; and they'll stick around, trying to push those buttons again and again.

When we let on that we're irritated, we actually bring more hardship on ourselves. That's why the writer of this verse says it's foolish to let others know right away that we're miffed. If we're wise, we'll keep our mouths shut and watch as the difficult person walks away in defeat.

Dear Father, help me know when to ignore an
insult, and give me the self-control to do it. Amen.

MUSTARD SEED

*"For truly, I say to you, if you have faith like
a grain of mustard seed, you will say to this
mountain, 'Move from here to there,' and it will
move, and nothing will be impossible for you."*

MATTHEW 17:20 ESV

Have you ever seen a mustard seed? It is one of the tiniest seeds. The mustard plant, with its small beginnings, takes root almost immediately and will eventually grow into a nine-foot plant. It's too big to be contained in an ordinary garden; it needs to be planted in a field somewhere.

Our faith is like that. We may feel that our faith is small and weak. But given a chance, it will take root and expand into something too big to be contained in our own souls. It will grow so large, in fact, that we must move outside our comfortable boundaries. If we have even a tiny amount of faith, let it take root. Watch and see the miracles that grow from such humble beginnings.

*Dear Father, I place my tiny amount of faith in
You. I trust You to cause it to take root and grow
into something strong and miraculous. Amen.*

HONOR GOD

Do you not know that your bodies are temples of the Holy Spirit, who is in you, whom you have received from God? You are not your own; you were bought at a price. Therefore honor God with your bodies.

1 CORINTHIANS 6:19–20 NIV

What does it mean to honor God with our bodies? Does it mean to eat right, exercise, and stay as fit and healthy as we can? Of course it does, but it also means so much more. When we honor God with our bodies, we make the conscious choice, every day, to serve Him with all we have.

Though our minds may be forgetful, though we may struggle with certain areas of competence, He still wants us to use those minds for Him. And though our bodies may be frail and afflicted, He still wants it all. He wants us to honor Him and serve Him with all we have, imperfect as it may be. God, who is perfect, will be glorified through our willingness to give Him everything.

Dear Father, I want to honor You with my imperfect mind and body. I'm completely Yours. Amen.

THE STRAIGHT PATH

Trust the LORD with all your heart, and don't depend on your own understanding. Remember the LORD in all you do, and he will give you success.

PROVERBS 3:5–6 NCV

Family relationships can be tricky. Familiarity often breeds contempt; and the people we're supposed to love the most can sometimes be the hardest people to love. When we find ourselves feeling lost—not knowing how in the world we're supposed to get along with these people we're related to—we can call on God. Lean on Him.

When we rely on our own limited, human understanding, we often act in pride, respond in anger, and cause more turmoil. But when we call on God before reacting, He will calm our spirits and give us wisdom. He will create a straight path for us and show us how to deal with each situation in a way that leads to harmony and peace.

Dear Father, I need help when it comes to dealing with my family. Give me wisdom and patience, and make my paths straight. Amen.

HUMAN NATURE

For you are still of the flesh. For while there is
jealousy and strife among you, are you not of the
flesh and behaving only in a human way? For when
one says, "I follow Paul," and another, "I follow
Apollos," are you not being merely human?

I Corinthians 3:3–4 esv

It's human nature to be jealous of what someone else has. It's also human nature to compete with others and to want to be right. But God calls us to slough off our human natures and take on the characteristics of Christ.

Why does it matter who makes more money, has a nicer home, or has better-behaved children, as long as we're doing our best to honor Christ? God has called each of us as ambassadors to represent His cause, and He's placed us where He can best use us. When we're envious of another's placement in life, we cling to our human nature, which only holds us back in our heavenly journey.

Dear Father, please remind me, daily, that
though You bless us all differently, You do
bless us all. Forgive me for feeling jealous
and competitive of others. Amen.

GOD'S WISDOM

"Call to me and I will answer you, and will tell you great and hidden things that you have not known."

JEREMIAH 33:3 ESV

When families operate the way they're supposed to, we end up caring immensely about the people we're related to—our parents, spouse, siblings, and children. The more we care, the more we worry about the futures of those we love.

We can worry about our children and what paths they'll take. We worry about our parents and their health issues. We worry about the great unknown that awaits us all. But when we call to God, He will calm our fears. He will give us the assurance that all will be well, or that He has things under control. His Holy Spirit will even reveal things to us that we couldn't have known without His prompting.

Thousands of people of faith will testify of doctor's visits that wouldn't have been scheduled without God's prompting, or about random phone calls that turned into life-changing events. Call on God. Trust Him. He will reveal the things we need to know for ourselves and for our families.

Dear Father, I call on You.
Give me wisdom. Amen.

IN GOD'S IMAGE

For God has not given us a spirit of timidity,
but of power and love and discipline.

2 TIMOTHY 1:7 NASB

We were made in God's image. We also have a sin nature. The God part of us is strong and powerful and loving. Timidity, or fear of social judgment, is not from God. It is a result of our sin nature and comes straight from Satan.

There is a war going on for our souls. God wants us to live successful, victorious lives filled with peace, joy, and love. Satan wants to destroy us any way he can. One of Satan's favorite tools he uses to destroy our peace is anxiety. He whispers self-doubt into our spirits, and we listen. We believe the lies, and we are crippled by them.

When anxiety takes over, we can remember it comes from Satan. Listen to God's voice: "You are strong, powerful, and more than capable of handling any problem that comes your way. You are a child of God, made in My image."

Dear Father, thank You for making me like You.
Help me recognize Satan's voice and disregard
it. I am Your child, not his. Amen.

IT GETS BETTER

Dear friends, do not be surprised at the fiery ordeal
that has come on you to test you, as though something
strange were happening to you. But rejoice inasmuch
as you participate in the sufferings of Christ, so that
you may be overjoyed when his glory is revealed.

1 PETER 4:12–13 NIV

If we're living for Christ, it seems like our lives should be easy. While it's true that God blesses those who follow Him, He never promised this life would be a field of daisies. As a matter of fact, He promised that in this life, we'll have many troubles.

He also promised to stay with us in the midst of our troubles. He promised to hold us up and give us strength. And He promised to give us wisdom when we ask.

Christ, God's own Son, suffered immense pain and persecution. When we go through hard things, we can rejoice in the kinship we have with Christ. And just as Christ overcame sin and death and was ultimately victorious, we will be overcomers too. Hang in there. It gets better.

> *Dear Father, thank You for the reminder*
> *that Christ suffered much more than I*
> *have, and that it gets better. Amen.*

WEALTH OF SPIRIT

*A little sleep, a little slumber, a little folding of
the hands to rest—and poverty will come on you
like a thief and scarcity like an armed man.*

PROVERBS 6:10–11 NIV

Everywhere you look, you'll find chances to join the
next get-rich-quick scheme. Whether it's an ad to
connect with a new pyramid sales platform, start
a new career, or invest in deep-sea treasure in the
Bahamas, there is no shortage of opportunities to
work a little and get paid a lot. Unfortunately, these
lucrative plans seldom pan out.

The truth is, God wants us to work hard for our
money. He knows the pitfalls of both laziness and
riches; and He knows, in the long run, our spirits will
be richer if we have to labor for our luxuries. Even
if we have money now, we won't keep it very long
if we spend our days lazing on a yacht somewhere.

God is all in favor of a well-earned break now
and then, but laziness leads to poverty. He wants
His children to have the wealth of spirit that comes
from work.

Dear Father, help me be a hard worker. Amen.

BE REAL WITH GOD

How deserted lies the city, once so full of people!
How like a widow is she, who once was great
among the nations! She who was queen among
the provinces has now become a slave.

LAMENTATIONS 1:1 NIV

In the book of Lamentations, the author, Jeremiah, laments. He weeps bitterly over what has been lost. He does not say, "Chin up, shoulders back." He does not put on a happy face and carry on.

Somewhere in the midst of our modern conveniences, our culture has lost the art of lament. We ask how others are doing, but we don't really expect them to answer honestly. "I'm fine, thank you. And you?" is the expected response.

But we can be real with God. He expects it. He demands it! When we are hurting or confused or angry, He wants us to tell Him. He longs for intimacy with us, and intimacy is not possible without honesty.

God knows the gamut of human emotions. He has felt them Himself. When we are troubled, we can go to Him with our heartache. He will listen. He will comfort. He will understand.

Dear Father, teach me to lament. Amen.

SACRIFICIAL GIVING

*Jesus looked up and saw the rich putting their
gifts into the offering box, and he saw a poor
widow put in two small copper coins. And
he said, "Truly, I tell you, this poor widow
has put in more than all of them. For they all
contributed out of their abundance, but she out
of her poverty put in all she had to live on."*

LUKE 21:1–4 ESV

While we may laud celebrities for giving millions to
this cause or that, God isn't impressed. He looks
at percentages. This widow gave more than those
who gave buckets of gold from their surplus. And
God took notice.

When money is tight and we don't know how
we'll make ends meet, perhaps we should ask God
what He wants us to give. Perhaps it's our time or
talent. Perhaps it's an amount of money that seems
impossible at the moment. When we give sacrificially, with pure motives, God is impressed—and
He will bless.

*Dear Father, show me what
You want me to give. Amen.*

OTHERS-FOCUSED

Dear friend, I pray that you may enjoy good
health and that all may go well with you,
even as your soul is getting along well.

3 JOHN 1:2 NIV

When we're ill or afflicted—*especially* when we're ill
or afflicted—it's easy to become very *me* centered.
Our bodies ache, and we just want to feel better.
One of the best ways to feel better and have our
spirits lifted is to focus on others.

Who do you know who needs prayer? Pray for
them. Reach out to them. Write cards and letters or
make phone calls. Send social media messages. Let
others know you're thinking of them and that you
care. This kind of selfless effort will boost someone
else's spirit and make their day. In the process, our
own spirits will be lifted as we forget, for a moment,
about our woes and focus on making someone else's
life better.

Dear Father, show me how I can reach
out to others today, how I can pray, and
how I can show Your love. Amen.

A HEAVY LOAD

*"Come to me, all you who are weary and burdened,
and I will give you rest. Take my yoke upon you
and learn from me, for I am gentle and humble
in heart, and you will find rest for your souls.
For my yoke is easy and my burden is light."*

MATTHEW 11:28–30 NIV

Anxiety is a heavy burden to carry, and it will absolutely wear us out. When we're weary and burdened, God invites us to come to Him. He will trade our heavy burdens for His light ones. He'll exchange our difficult yoke for His easy one. And He will give us the rest we need.

Life is long. Some might say life is filled with hardship, and they would be correct. But the fact that life is long is also a blessing, because at every turn we find new opportunities, new chances, and new beginnings. With each step, God offers to take our hefty loads and replace them with tranquility, peace, and joy.

Dear Father, I'm carrying such a heavy load right now. Please take it from me, and give me rest. Amen.

DIVINE HEALING

And Jesus said to him, "Go your way; your
faith has made you well." And immediately he
recovered his sight and followed him on the way.

MARK 10:52 ESV

This story of faith healing a person's physical ailment
has often been misrepresented. God is perfectly
capable of healing our infirmities and diseases. But
our physical health is *not* God's top priority. Instead,
our *spiritual* health is at the top of God's list of goals
for each of our lives.

Each of us who knows Christ as our Savior will
ultimately be healed. One day, when we arrive
in heaven, we will be issued new bodies, and we
won't have any more pain for all eternity. It's our
spiritual health that determines whether we will be
allowed into heaven or not. And it's our spiritual
health that affects those around us most. When
we have a physical ailment, it is appropriate to ask
God to heal us; but if He doesn't answer the way
we want, we need to take a closer look. Perhaps
He's using that ailment to heal our spirits, or the
spirits of those around us.

Dear Father, heal me. I trust You. Amen.

CLING TO HOPE

Bitterly she weeps at night, tears are on her cheeks. Among all her lovers there is no one to comfort her. All her friends have betrayed her; they have become her enemies.

LAMENTATIONS 1:2 NIV

Have you ever felt abandoned and forgotten? We've all felt that way at times. The people we thought we could trust prove untrustworthy. Those we considered our closest allies betray us. When that happens, our souls ache in the deepest part of us. We may feel like things will never turn around, like all hope is lost.

We don't need to feel that way, though. God is a God of hope; and hope is the opposite of fear. Fear is a belief that something bad will happen, and hope is the belief that something good will happen. As long as we have God, we have hope, because He never, ever runs out of goodness.

Dear Father, right now it feels like nothing will ever be better. Yet I will cling to the belief that You have good things in store for my life. Amen.

A BOUNTIFUL HARVEST

*The hardworking farmer should be the
first to receive a share of the crops.*

2 TIMOTHY 2:6 NIV

When reading this verse, many of us will bob our
heads in agreement. Of course the farmer should
be the first to enjoy his own harvest! But we can't
overlook the adjective in the first part of the verse:
hardworking. The farmer who works hard should
receive the first share of the crops.

But what about the lazy farmer? He will rarely
receive the first share, because bill collectors and
creditors will stand at the door, waiting to receive
payment before the farmer can even haul in the
goods. Even if he has worked hard for a few weeks,
any laxity in the past might have caused the bills to
pile up.

This verse is a principle, not a promise. Sometimes, circumstances beyond our control cause
financial hardship in spite of our hard work. But
when we make hard work a habit, over time, we will
reap a bountiful harvest.

> *Dear Father, help me to make hard work a
> habit, like the productive farmer. Amen.*

FULL OF COMPASSION

The LORD is a refuge for the oppressed,
a stronghold in times of trouble.

PSALM 9:9 NIV

God is full of compassion. The word *compassion* means to have passion with and for another person. God is passionate *for* us! He has passion *with* us. That means when we are in trouble, when we're hurting, when we feel lost and alone. . .He feels every bit of our pain just as passionately as we do.

He is all-powerful, and He uses that power on our behalf when we reach out to Him. His care for us won't allow Him to do anything else! When it seems life's storms will blow us away, we can simply call His name. He will never leave us nor forsake us. He will be there, sheltering us, protecting us, and giving us strength. He is our refuge and our stronghold, and He will not let us go.

Dear Father, thank You for being passionate about me. I need You now. I know You are my refuge and my stronghold, and I will cling to You. Amen.

THE LOVE OF MONEY

The love of money causes all kinds of evil.
Some people have left the faith, because
they wanted to get more money, but they
have caused themselves much sorrow.

1 TIMOTHY 6:10 NCV

This principle is often misunderstood. Money is not the root of all kinds of evil. Money is inanimate. It has no soul. Rather, the *love* of money is the source of all kinds of evil. The source isn't our bank accounts or the size of our wallets—it's our hearts.

Our hearts will run after the thing we love the most. If we love money, we will pursue it with a passion, whether by stealing it or cheating to get it or working long hours at the expense of our families. But when we love God most, we pursue righteousness and a godly life. We pursue faith, gentleness, and love. The interest earned from a godly life is far greater than any amount of money.

Dear Father, I want to pursue You. Amen.

GOD WILL HELP YOU

"For I am the LORD your God who takes
hold of your right hand and says to
you, Do not fear; I will help you."

ISAIAH 41:13 NIV

Most small children are absolutely at ease when they are near a parent. If something scares them, they can run to that parent and know they are safe. As long as they are holding a parent's hand, they know everything will be okay.

God wants us to have that kind of faith in Him. Like a loving parent, He reaches out His hand to us and says, "Don't be afraid. I'm right here, and I'll help you." Whenever we feel anxious, we can pump our right hand open and closed and picture Him holding it firmly in His grip. We can know that no matter what we face, He is right there with us, giving us wisdom and strength and power.

Dear Father, I don't know why it's so easy to forget You're right here with me. Thank You for holding my hand and helping me through each situation I face. Amen.

HEAVEN ON EARTH

One thing have I asked of the LORD, that will I seek after: that I may dwell in the house of the LORD all the days of my life, to gaze upon the beauty of the LORD and to inquire in his temple.

PSALM 27:4 ESV

Can you imagine what heaven will be like? Living in God's presence—where sin cannot exist—will be glorious on so many levels. No violence, no harsh words, no judgment. . .only love, peace, joy, and total acceptance.

While we can't duplicate heaven on earth, that should always be our goal. When we speak gently, when we love boundlessly, when we do all we can to live at peace with those in our household. . .we create a little haven, a piece of heaven on earth. Showing love and acceptance to those who don't live up to our standards is hard, yet that's what God does every time He looks at us.

Dear Father, help me create a bit of heaven on earth. I want to love like You love. Amen.

WORTH IT

*"Blessed are those who are persecuted for
righteousness' sake, for theirs is the kingdom of
heaven. Blessed are you when others revile you
and persecute you and utter all kinds of evil against
you falsely on my account. Rejoice and be glad,
for your reward is great in heaven, for so they
persecuted the prophets who were before you."*

MATTHEW 5:10–12 ESV

One of the worst things we can endure is the experience of doing the right thing and getting persecuted for it. When doing the wrong thing earns people esteem and praise, and doing the noble thing earns us nothing more than mocking and jeers, it pretty much stinks.

But God says not to worry! He sees. He knows. And He promises great blessings on those who endure persecution for His sake. Persecution can come in many forms, but it is never pleasant. God wants us to remember that though we may endure some hard things, He will make it worth it in the end.

*Dear Father, please comfort the persecuted
Christians around the world right now.
Help me stand by my convictions,
even when it's hard. Amen.*

HE IS NEAR

*My eyes fail because of tears, my spirit is
greatly troubled; my heart is poured out
on the earth because of the destruction
of the daughter of my people.*

LAMENTATIONS 2:11 NASB

It's a familiar scene, though it's one we rarely talk about in public. We cry ourselves to sleep, or we don't sleep at all. We simply cry the night away, turning our pillows to the dry side, only to soak that side as well.

God doesn't leave us alone with our tears. He is right there with us. Psalm 56:8 even tells us He records our misery and heartache. He counts every single tear and keeps a list! He does that because He cares so deeply. Our tears are every bit as precious to Him as money is to a banker.

When our eyes ache because of all the crying, we can reach out to Him and feel His presence—for that's when we know He is near.

*Dear Father, thank You for not leaving
me alone in my sorrow. Amen.*

MORE THAN CONQUERORS

No temptation has overtaken you that is not
common to man. God is faithful, and he will
not let you be tempted beyond your ability, but
with the temptation he will also provide the way
of escape, that you may be able to endure it.
1 CORINTHIANS 10:13 ESV

Ask any bodybuilder. The only way to build bigger, stronger muscles is to continue pushing to the limit. The phrase "no pain, no gain" is true, if we want physical growth. The same is true for our spiritual growth.

Sometimes, it may seem God has led us into a situation where we're destined to fail, but that's not true. When God allows us to go through something, it's because He has faith in us! He knows that with Him beside us, we're ready to handle whatever life throws our way. He will not lead us into sure failure. Instead, He leads us into the opportunity to be more than conquerors in this life.

Dear Father, I trust You. Help me to be more than
a conqueror in my current situation. Amen.

ALL FOR THE GLORY

*So whether you eat or drink or whatever
you do, do it all for the glory of God.*
1 CORINTHIANS 10:31 NIV

Many of us don't mind giving God the glory, as long as things are going the way we want them to. But when our lives take a sudden detour and we end up on a path we didn't plan for or want, we often try to take over the steering wheel. We want to take control and set our lives back on the path we mapped out for ourselves.

But part of becoming mature is the simple willingness to give up control, allow God to do whatever He wants in our lives, and praise Him in the process. When we move aside and allow Him to have His way, He will do wonderful and amazing things in our lives and take us on an adventure we could never imagine.

Dear Father, forgive me for wanting to control my life. I give You permission to do whatever You want. Whatever comes, I will glorify You. Amen.

THE CENTER OF YOUR THOUGHTS

Keep your lives free from the love of money, and be satisfied with what you have. God has said, "I will never leave you; I will never abandon you."

HEBREWS 13:5 NCV

We often associate the love of money with the rich. We think those who have a lot of money must love it, and they must be corrupt. But the love of money has very little to do with how much of it we have. It has *everything* to do with our hearts.

When we're struggling to make ends meet, it's easy to become fixated on money. *How will I make more of it? How can I spend it? How can I save it? What expenses might I cut so I can pay my bills? How would I splurge if I had plenty of money?* These questions and concerns are not evil, but they can become obsessive. Rich or poor, it's important to remember God wants us to keep *Him*, not money, in the center of our thoughts. It is God, not money, who will provide for us and meet our needs.

Dear Father, help me be wise with my money and with my thoughts. Amen.

111

WHEN YOU ARE AFRAID

When I am afraid, I put my trust in you.
PSALM 56:3 NIV

This short verse is easy enough for even the most stubborn mind to memorize. It's a mantra and can become a mental chant for anytime we feel anxious and afraid. God loves us more than we can imagine, and He wants only good for us. When we truly place our trust in Him, He helps us. He gives us wisdom and confidence.

Job interview? No problem. *When I am afraid, I will trust in You.* Mean people? Piece of cake. *When I am afraid, I will trust in You.* New, frightening situation? Scary illness? Worries about the future? *When I am afraid, I will trust in You.* God loves us, and He will never let us down. When we feel like the cares of this world are just too much to bear, we can remember this verse, remember His love, and relax.

Dear Father, thank You for this simple reminder that I don't have to be afraid of anything. I can transfer all my fears to You, and You will take care of me. I trust You. Amen.

A JOB WELL DONE

*The LORD God took the man and put him in the
Garden of Eden to work it and take care of it.*

GENESIS 2:15 NIV

We often want to blame Adam and Eve's sin for the
fact that we now have to work hard. While their
poor choice did have a far-reaching effect, it's not
the reason we must labor. God placed Adam in the
garden to work it and take care of it before the fall.
Before the serpent. *Before* Eve ate that stinkin' fruit.

God created us in His image. He gained immense
satisfaction from creating the earth and everything in
it. He wants us to enjoy that same sense of purpose
that comes from a job well done. He gave us work
as a gift, not a punishment.

He wants us to be able to step back at the end of
the day or the end of a project and say, "I did this,
and it's good." He wants us to sleep hard, knowing
we added value to the lives of those around us. He
loves us; and believe it or not, that's why He gives
us work to do.

Dear Father, thank You for work. Amen.

BE AN ENCOURAGER

Encourage one another.

HEBREWS 10:25 NLT

Wouldn't it be nice if, just once, Christ called us to do the easy thing? Instead, He calls us to do what others don't want to do. We are to love our enemies, bless those who curse us, and encourage those who verbally and emotionally beat us down. How in the world are we supposed to do that?

The truth is, God wants to take us to a place beyond ourselves. He wants us to live on a higher plane. When we surrender to His will for our lives and say, "I can't do it, God, but I know You can," He works miracles. He changes our hearts, and He often changes the hearts of those around us. Often, that change begins with an encouraging word to another person, even when it's the last thing we want to do. When we encourage others, God begins a cycle of love that will come back to us many times over.

Dear Father, help me be an encourager! Amen.

LOVING FATHER

*For my father and my mother have
forsaken me, but the LORD will take me in.*

PSALM 27:10 ESV

Rejection is hard, no matter where it comes from. But when we're rejected by members of our own family—the people who are supposed to love us most—the sting is especially bitter. God set us in families to keep us from being lonely, but families don't always work the way God intended.

God is a loving, compassionate Father. He is generous. He is kind. He is faithful and constant, and He will never leave us nor forsake us. No matter how lonely we feel on this earth, we are never alone. In Jesus, we have a Savior, an advocate, and a cheerleader. He offers His love freely; and if we ask, He will even provide other people in this world to fill in where our families have let us down.

Dear Father, thank You for loving me, accepting me, and being my Father. Thank You for taking me in. Give me a family to be a part of, and help me offer that kind of love to others as well. Amen.

FIRM STEPS

The LORD makes firm the steps of the one who
delights in him; though he may stumble, he will
not fall, for the LORD upholds him with his hand.
PSALM 37:23–24 NIV

God is thrilled when He sees us trying to follow Him and do His will. He cares more about our hearts than about perfection. He is not disillusioned by our mistakes and failures; He never had any illusions about us to begin with. He simply sees His child, who is trying to please Him, and He is delighted.

When we reach out to Him, He takes hold of our hands and guides us. But if we want that kind of support from God, we must be sure to seek His advice before stepping out. We must do as He says, and He will help us. It is our humble acknowledgment of Him as Lord that brings His favor on our lives.

Dear Father, I want to delight You. I want to
follow You, and I humbly seek Your guidance
for each step I take. Thank You for holding
me up and making my steps firm. Amen.

ANSWER TO GOD

*Every person is to be in subjection to the governing
authorities. For there is no authority except from
God, and those which exist are established by God.*

ROMANS 13:1 NASB

It's easy to understand why we should respect authority when that authority is good and righteous and just. But what about corrupt authority? What if our ruler or governor or president isn't someone we like or respect? What if he or she exhibits anything but godliness? What if our boss treats employees with disrespect, shows little compassion, gossips, slanders, and belittles them at every opportunity?

God says we're still to respect their position. We're to respect the fact that God placed them in that position—or at least, He allows them to be there. When we honor authority, we're really honoring God. The evil ruler or the unfair boss will answer to God for each action. . .just as the rest of us will.

*Dear Father, help me treat authority figures with
honor and respect, even when I don't feel it. I do
so out of respect for You, not them. Amen.*

PERFECT LOVE

There is no fear in love. But perfect love drives
out fear, because fear has to do with punishment.
The one who fears is not made perfect in love.

1 John 4:18 niv

Anyone who struggles with anxiety knows it can creep into every area of our lives. Once fear gets a foothold, its voice is louder than logic, stronger than good sense. We must learn to recognize anxiety's voice: it is Satan, the father of lies.

Anxiety tells us we can't. Love—which comes from God—tells us we can, and He will help us. Anxiety whispers, "You're not enough." God proclaims, "You are treasured and adored. You are so valuable, I gave My Son for you. You are more than enough." Anxiety pushes our head downward; love lifts our chin.

Anxiety makes us cowardly; love makes us confident—not in ourselves, but in our Creator's purpose in us. Whenever we feel afraid, we can remind ourselves of the source of that fear, call on our Father who loves us, and watch fear flee.

Dear Father, thank You for Your exquisite, tender
love for me. Thank You for driving out fear. Amen.

RELATIONSHIPS BEFORE WORK

In his defense Jesus said to them,
"My Father is always at his work to this
very day, and I too am working."

JOHN 5:17 NIV

Isn't it great to know God is always working on our behalf? He never takes a break from His love for us. This doesn't mean He never rests. But His mind is always in motion for us. The heart of His existence is always on relationships.

It's easy to get distracted with work and forget about our relationships. But God designed us to connect with other people. When we neglect time with family, friends, and others who need us so that we can pursue money, things go horribly wrong. God wants us to work, but He doesn't want us to forget the reason we work. We work for Him, yes. But we also work to provide a good, stable life for the people we care about. Let the work that we *continuously* do be for our relationships, not our salaries.

Dear Father, remind me to work toward
good, positive relationships in my life more
than I work for money. Amen.

WORKING OUT

*For physical training is of some value, but
godliness has value for all things, holding promise
for both the present life and the life to come.*

1 TIMOTHY 4:8 NIV

Aside from true athletes and fitness buffs, most of us don't relish the idea of working out. It's hard. It takes time. And it makes us sweat. But if we want to be healthy and fit, we do it anyway. Exercise keeps our muscles and bones strong, improves our mind function, and relieves stress.

Exercise may have countless benefits for our physical bodies, but the benefits of godly living are even greater for every aspect of our lives. When we live according to God's standards, our relationships are more peaceful. We excel in our jobs. We avoid dangerous physical and emotional pitfalls. Though we can't control everything that happens to us physically, spiritually, and emotionally, we can put forth our best effort to live a godly life.

Dear Father, thank You for the wisdom found in Your Word. I want to do all I can to be godly. Amen.

LOVE AND PRAY

"But I say to you, love your enemies and pray for those who persecute you, so that you may be sons of your Father who is in heaven; for He causes His sun to rise on the evil and the good, and sends rain on the righteous and the unrighteous. For if you love those who love you, what reward do you have? Do not even the tax collectors do the same?"

MATTHEW 5:44–46 NASB

Any parent who has more than one child will tell you they love each child equally. They may love them differently, based on different personalities, but the amount of love is the same, and it's unending.

God loves us that way. Though some of His children may be more pleasing, more obedient, more compassionate and loving, He doesn't love the disagreeable children any less. Because we're made in God's image, He wants us to love like He loves! He longs for us to love even those people who are difficult to love. If we ask Him, He will give us the will and the desire to love—and pray for—even our enemies.

Dear Father, help me love and pray for my enemies. Amen.

GREAT IS GOD'S FAITHFULNESS

Yet this I call to mind and therefore I have hope:
Because of the LORD's great love we are not
consumed, for his compassions never fail. They are
new every morning; great is your faithfulness.

LAMENTATIONS 3:21–23 NIV

When Jeremiah wrote the book of Lamentations, he was as sad, distraught, and heartbroken as anyone can be. He had watched his friends and family make poor choices, and those poor choices led to their destruction. He had lost everyone he loved.

Yet when he searched deep in his soul, he found hope. He knew that, no matter how bad things get, God is good. God is compassionate. And God is faithful.

No matter how hopeless things may seem, we can follow Jeremiah's example. We can weep and wail and cry, knowing God holds us in His arms, comforting us, caring for us. We can know He cries with us. And we can be assured that His ultimate goodness will prevail.

Dear Father, I know You are good, even when
my circumstances aren't. Thank You for Your
compassion. Remind me of Your love, and
help me find hope again. Amen.

THE LIVING WORD OF GOD

*So faith comes from hearing, and
hearing through the word of Christ.*

ROMANS 10:17 ESV

When we find ourselves in a crisis of faith, we often look everywhere for answers. We listen to wise gurus of this way of thinking or that way of thinking. We read self-help books. We may even start a new exercise plan. Unfortunately, the place that can help us grow in our faith is often the last place we look—God's Word.

One of the great things about God's Word is that it never changes. So the same words that strengthened Abraham and Paul and even Mary will strengthen us. But just as a jar of vitamins won't do us any good unopened on a shelf, God's Word must be read and absorbed into our thoughts before it will grow our faith.

Next time we find ourselves wondering if God is real, we can find our answers in the pages of the Bible, God's living Word.

*Dear Father, help me to read and
understand Your Word today. Amen.*

PATIENTLY WAITING

Wait for the LORD; be strong, and let your heart take courage; wait for the LORD!

PSALM 27:14 ESV

One of the greatest qualities a person can have is patience. It's also one of the hardest character traits to develop; and it's the one thing that can't be rushed. Patience requires gentle waiting, and none of us likes to wait.

When it comes to family relationships, patience can make all the difference in the dynamics of a home. When we're patient with others' shortcomings—realizing we are all works in progress and God is actively shaping us into the people He created us to be—we set up an atmosphere of peace and acceptance. In contrast, when we become easily irritated with others' flaws, we generate a toxic environment that makes it difficult for anyone to thrive.

God is immensely patient with us. When we're tempted to lose our patience with others, we should remember to gently wait as God brings about His divine purpose in their lives.

Dear Father, thank You for being patient with me. Teach me to be patient with others, knowing You are working in their lives. Amen.

HE IS WITH YOU

*"So do not fear, for I am with you; do not
be dismayed, for I am your God. I will
strengthen you and help you; I will uphold
you with my righteous right hand."*

ISAIAH 41:10 NIV

Depression is no respecter of persons. It doesn't matter if you're rich or poor; highbrow or blue collar; black, white, or brown skinned. Depression will suck the life right out of a person. But depression won't win, as long as we trust God to see us through. He will strengthen us, help us, and hold us up.

Sometimes He provides help through trusted friends we can talk to. Sometimes He might provide needed medication. He will *always* provide a listening ear and all the love in His heart. When you feel like depression will win, look in the mirror and remind yourself that nothing is stronger than Almighty God. And God is in your corner.

Dear Father, thank You for holding me up and giving me strength. Please help me beat this depression. I love You. I trust You. I know You are good. Amen.

ON GREED

Then Jesus said to them, "Be careful and guard against all kinds of greed. Life is not measured by how much one owns."

LUKE 12:15 NCV

Living life by comparison—that is, measuring our success by how much we have, compared to others—has always been an issue. Social media has compounded the problem, because many of us share what we want others to see and hide what we want to keep secret. This causes us to think everyone else's lives are better than ours, for we only see the best parts of their existence. Often, what we see is carefully staged and doesn't represent reality.

Jealousy over what we think others have can cause us to be greedy. We want to measure up to our peers, so we purchase more stuff. But money and things never satisfy for long. True happiness comes from healthy relationships with God and others. Greed draws our attention away from the very thing that will bring us lasting fulfillment.

Dear Father, forgive me for being greedy. Help me to focus on love—for You and for others. Amen.

YOU'RE HIS

But now, this is what the LORD says—he who created you, Jacob, he who formed you, Israel: "Do not fear, for I have redeemed you; I have summoned you by name; you are mine."

ISAIAH 43:1 NIV

Anxiety makes us feel alone, even in a crowd. With anxiety as our partner, we feel isolated and invisible. But anxiety is wrong! Don't listen to it. Anxiety's native language is lies.

Think of that feeling of isolation, of loneliness in a throng of people. Now recall the beauty of hearing a familiar voice call you by name. Hear the delight in that voice, because the owner is thrilled to see you and be in your presence. *That* is God's voice, and it happens every moment. He calls us by name. He says, "Here, sit by Me. I saved this place of honor for you." He says, "I'm so glad you're Mine."

Next time you feel afraid, tell your pounding heart to be still and listen. You'll hear Him, calling you by name. Proclaiming His care for you. Reminding you that you're special, you're loved, and you're His.

Dear Father, thank You for calling me by name. Amen.

CHOICES

*My child, listen to your father's teaching
and do not forget your mother's advice.
Their teaching will be like flowers in your
hair or a necklace around your neck.*

PROVERBS 1:8–9 NCV

Some things just go together: salt and pepper, peanut butter and jelly, worry and parenting. It's too bad children aren't born with a detailed instruction manual attached to their umbilical cords. "Do X, Y, and Z and in twenty years you'll have a healthy, well-adjusted, successful adult." Instead, we do the best we can, and we pray a lot. And, of course, we worry.

The bottom line is, our children are individuals. They make their own decisions and choose their own paths. We can teach them, train them, model righteous living for them. . .but it is up to them whether they hear that teaching and make it part of their lives. The command in the above verse is to children, not parents. We must do our part as parents to lovingly teach and train. Then we must let our children make their own choices.

*Dear Father, I release my child to You.
Help me not to worry. Amen.*

GOOD COMPANY

*"Remember the word that I said to you: 'A
servant is not greater than his master.' If they
persecuted me, they will also persecute you. If
they kept my word, they will also keep yours."*

JOHN 15:20 ESV

Wisdom tells us that if someone will gossip about
or slander another person when they are with us,
they will probably gossip about or slander us when
they're out of our presence. In this verse, Christ
urges His followers to remember this. If someone has
persecuted you, they've done it to others as well; and
they'd do it Christ Himself, given the opportunity.

While we can't avoid difficult people altogether,
we should show wisdom in selecting our close friends.
If a person consistently treats others with kindness
and respect, chances are, they will treat us that way
too. We should also remember when enduring harsh
treatment from others, that Christ was treated harshly
as well. We are in good company.

*Dear Father, give me wisdom in selecting
my friends. Help me be a trustworthy
friend to others as well. Amen.*

PEACE WITHIN

"Peace be within your walls and security within your towers!" For my brothers and companions' sake I will say, "Peace be within you!"

PSALM 122:7–8 ESV

It's God's desire that we live in peace with ourselves and others. Unfortunately, we live in a fallen, broken world where peace seems elusive. Yet we can know, without doubt, that God longs for us to experience the peace that only comes from Him.

It's interesting that the psalmist starts by saying, "Peace be within your walls," and ends by saying, "Peace be within you!" Truly, as the old song says, peace on earth does begin within each of us. Even when everything around us feels like a war, God has given us every tool we need to live at peace with Him and others. When life feels anything but peaceful, we can remember that peace doesn't come from without. . .it comes from within.

Dear Father, show me Your peace. When life is chaotic and people around me are mean, remind me of Your presence. Amen.

CRY OUT!

The righteous cry out, and the LORD hears them;
he delivers them from all their troubles.

PSALM 34:17 NIV

God is always listening to us, waiting for us to call on Him. He never falls asleep, and He never goes off duty. When we cry out to Him, He hears, and He delivers us! He will never turn a deaf ear to His children; He will not ignore our pleas for help.

If we didn't have troubles, we wouldn't need Him to deliver us. If we didn't endure hardship, we might forget all about Him. God doesn't cause the bad things in our lives; but He allows them, and He uses them to shape us into the loving, compassionate, wise people He wants us to be. He also allows them because He longs for our attention, and He knows we might not call on Him if we didn't have a need.

Dear Father, thank You for hearing me
when I cry out. I need You to deliver me,
and I know that You will. Amen.

HOPE IN THE LORD

The LORD is good to those whose hope is in
him, to the one who seeks him; it is good to
wait quietly for the salvation of the LORD.

LAMENTATIONS 3:25–26 NIV

Hope is the firm belief that good things will happen. It is not a flimsy fairy-tale wish, but a steadfast conviction. God is good. He is *only* good. When we live in Him, good things will come to us. When we seek Him desperately—when we look for Him with relentless resolve, when we search for Him with every last drop of our being—we will find Him. And that is where every good thing dwells.

More than anything, God wants our devotion. He wants our time and attention. He wants to fill our thoughts. He does not withhold goodness from us in some kind of horse-and-carrot trick; instead, He waits for us, ready to shower His kindness on all who seek His presence. His goodness is an invitation to share His company.

Dear Father, I seek You. I long for Your
presence. I want to live inside Your goodness.
You are my hope, Lord. I love You. Amen.

A GOOD FATHER

Then Jesus answered her, "O woman, great is
your faith! Be it done for you as you desire."
And her daughter was healed instantly.
MATTHEW 15:28 ESV

Wouldn't it be great if God did everything we asked, simply because we asked? Why, we'd all be healthy and wealthy and beautiful. We would want for nothing. . .which means we'd eventually stop coming to God for anything.

God is a good Father. And like any good father, He longs to give us what we ask for. But sometimes His answer is no. Sometimes, He has a different plan for our lives than the plan we've mapped out for ourselves.

Sometimes, though, His answer is yes! We may never know the possibilities of His generosity if we don't ask. When we have a need, or even a want, He longs for us to come to Him. No matter His answer, He will always pour out His love.

Dear Father, You know my needs. You know
my desires. Please answer my prayers, for
You are the only one who can. Amen.

PRINCIPLE OR PROMISE?

*Start children off on the way they should go, and
even when they are old they will not turn from it.*

PROVERBS 22:6 NIV

This verse sounds like a promise, doesn't it? If it
were, we'd have a lot less heartache in this world.
Many people are taught right from wrong, shown
the best path, and trained to live godly, principled
lives. But that doesn't negate the fact that every
person in this world is given the right to choose. It
is a right given by God; and that right leaves room
for poor choices as well as wise ones.

However, when we diligently teach our children
the way they should go, we greatly increase the
odds that they will grow into decent, God-fearing,
righteous adults. This verse is a principle, not a
promise. Yet it is a principle that wise parents will
persistently adhere to. It is a principle that, more
often than not, will prove true and lead to a joy-
filled, peace-filled life for those who will listen.

*Dear Father, help me to consistently, persistently
teach my children Your ways. Amen.*

A DIFFERENT PATH

Finally, brothers and sisters, whatever is true, whatever is noble, whatever is right, whatever is pure, whatever is lovely, whatever is admirable—if anything is excellent or praiseworthy—think about such things.

PHILIPPIANS 4:8 NIV

Have you ever known a toxic person? Have you ever *been* a toxic person? Toxic people are negative, discouraging, and judgmental. But they are also often witty and intelligent, and their deceptive charm can suck us in before we know it. Soon, our thoughts mirror theirs, and we're negative, gossipy, and mean. . . and we wonder why we're in a bad mood all the time.

Paul encourages us to take a different path. He wants our thoughts to center around the good, the noble, the true. He wants us to think about things that are pure, excellent, and praiseworthy. He wants our contemplations to rest in the admirable, the kind, the gentle, the compassionate. When we discipline our minds to focus on the positive, our spirits are lifted from the muck. In turn, we lift those around us.

Dear Father, keep my mind focused on positive, noble thoughts today. Help me lift others up. Amen.

SUPERPOWER

*Jesus called his twelve disciples to him
and gave them authority to drive out impure
spirits and to heal every disease and sickness.*

MATTHEW 10:1 NIV

Many of us read this verse and wonder what was so special about the disciples, that they could cast out evil spirits and heal diseases. We wonder why we don't have the same abilities today. The truth is, God didn't give the disciples any special gifts or talents in that area. He did give them power—a very special superpower—and he's given us the same power. That power is the Holy Spirit.

The problem is, many of us have watched a few too many superhero movies. We expect instant results; but God often has a greater purpose in the situations we encounter. His purpose is accomplished, more often than not, over time and with much perseverance. When we encounter a situation that needs healing, we need only to call on the power He's already given us, wait for Him to act, and trust Him with the results.

*Dear Father, teach me to use Your power
effectively. I love You. Amen.*

ENCOURAGING LAYERS

But you, LORD, are a shield around me,
my glory, the One who lifts my head high.
PSALM 3:3 NIV

When we dissect this verse, we find many encouraging layers. First, God is a shield around us. A shield is normally held in front of a warrior to protect him from bullets or arrows. But God isn't just in front of us—He *surrounds* us! He protects us from every side. When we stay close to Him, He will shield us from Satan's arrows.

He also bestows glory on us. When we feel insignificant, we can know that God loves to receive glory. He made us to be like Him, and He knows we need to shine as well. He has plans for us to have our moments in the sun; He will give us glory.

When we feel ashamed, He lifts our heads. When we ask for forgiveness and truly repent—or turn away—from our sins, He places a hand under our chin and lifts our faces to Him. Once He's forgiven us, we have nothing to be ashamed of. We are clean.

Dear Father, thank You for this reminder. Amen.

STAYING BUSY AT WORK

*Make it your ambition to lead a quiet life: You
should mind your own business and work
with your hands, just as we told you.*

1 THESSALONIANS 4:11 NIV

One of the biggest headaches bosses complain about
is workplace drama. It has little to do with the actual
work that's required by employees. Workplace drama
is the watercooler gossip, the slander, the backbiting
that occurs when people are supposed to be working,
but aren't.

In this verse, Paul encourages his readers to stay
away from the watercooler! He wants us to do our
jobs and mind our own business. When we stay
busy doing what we're supposed to be doing, we
avoid the type of histrionics that occurs as a result of
idle gossip. When we stay busy, we actually get our
work done in a positive way, which leads to success
in the workplace.

*Dear Father, help me avoid workplace drama and
gossip. When I interact with others, remind me to be
positive and encouraging. Help me to concentrate
on doing my job the best I can do it. Amen.*

ALL MY NEEDS

And my God will supply all your needs according
to His riches in glory in Christ Jesus.
PHILIPPIANS 4:19 NASB

How often do we stress over how this need or that one will be met? Whether it's a bill that needs to be paid, a piece of clothing we need for an event, or a relationship that will fill an empty space in our hearts, God will provide! He has a vast storehouse of treasures, and He wants us to trust Him. He longs to delight His children—particularly when we relax in Him, believing He will supply all our needs.

When we have a need, we should tell God about it and then leave it with Him. Our lives become a beautiful, exciting treasure hunt when we make our requests known with full confidence that He'll deliver. He is God. He will provide. And when He does, it will be more than we need.

Dear Father, forgive me for worrying
about my needs. I know You will
provide, and I trust You. Amen.

FAITH WITHOUT DOUBT

And Jesus answered them, "Truly, I say to you,
if you have faith and do not doubt, you will not
only do what has been done to the fig tree, but
even if you say to this mountain, 'Be taken up
and thrown into the sea,' it will happen."

MATTHEW 21:21 ESV

This is an interesting story of our Lord. Jesus was traveling. He was hungry. He saw a fig tree and stopped for a snack. But there were no figs on the tree, so Jesus cursed it and said it would never bear fruit again. Immediately, the tree withered.

When His disciples questioned Him about why the tree withered so fast, Jesus essentially said, "You have this kind of power at your fingertips." Faith, when it's not mixed with doubt, is potent stuff. Faith unleashes the power of God in our lives. There is no end to what God can and will do through a person whose faith in Him is pure.

Dear Father, teach me to have the kind of
faith You talked about. I believe. Amen.

REWARDS BEYOND MEASURE

*Don't grumble against one another,
brothers and sisters.*

JAMES 5:9 NIV

Any parent who has more than one child knows that siblings fight. It's just a fact of life. Childhood is filled with brothers and sisters, grumbling and groaning about what he said or she did and how it's not fair. But as we grow and develop, those childish arguments *should* give way to a deep-reaching love. Siblings, when mature, can be the best of friends.

James warns us against acting like children. We are brothers and sisters in Christ, but we are called to be mature. There is no room in the Christian life for petty, childish grumbling. We are supposed to encourage one another, to give generously, and to love deeply. The rewards of this kind of well-developed affection are beyond measure.

Dear Father, forgive me for grumbling against my brothers and sisters in Christ, even if it's just in my heart. Help me to show kindness and compassion, and to love others with a mature love. Amen.

BLESSINGS, NOW AND THEN

He brought them forth also with silver and gold: and there was not one feeble person among their tribes.
PSALM 105:37 KJV

This verse brings forth an *I'll-have-what-they're-having* sense of wonder. Just what was it about these people that caused God to bless them with both health and riches? What this verse doesn't show, however, is that those earthly blessings were not permanent. Each of those people did eventually die; and when they did, they did not take their silver and gold with them.

God wants to bless us today. He sent His Son, Jesus, so we could have abundant life. But the blessings of eternity are so much greater than anything we can imagine in the here and now. When God doesn't choose to answer our prayers for more money or replenished health, He's not ignoring our requests; He's just answering them differently. When we join His presence in heaven, we will have silver and gold, and there will not be one feeble person among us.

Dear Father, thank You for the blessings You give me in this life. Remind me of the blessings that await me in eternity. Amen.

IT TAKES FAITH

Cast all your anxiety on him,
because he cares for you.

1 PETER 5:7 NRSV

Anxiety can leave us frozen, unable to react or respond to the fear that consumes us. This little verse reminds us that when we feel anxious and afraid, we can fight back. It doesn't say that if we do nothing, God will take our anxiety away. We must act. We must *throw* our anxiety onto God. It isn't a toss or a flick, but a *throw*. We must put our weight behind the action and heft all our anxiety onto Him.

It takes faith to do that. When God sees us using all our energy, in faith, to cast our cares onto Him, He reacts in love. He catches it all in His great arms and takes it off our hands. He cares about us; and as He intervenes on our behalf, He will give us peace and confidence and a serenity we can't describe.

Dear Father, thank You for this reminder not
to let my anxiety consume me; but rather, to
take charge and throw it onto You. Amen.

FOR THE LORD'S SAKE

Submit yourselves for the Lord's sake to every human institution, whether to a king as the one in authority, or to governors as sent by him for the punishment of evildoers and the praise of those who do right.

1 PETER 2:13–14 NASB

When we submit to the authority of human government and institutions, we do so *for the Lord's sake*, because He asked us to. Most laws are created for the good of mankind. Upholding the law keeps our society organized and safe. We may not agree with every rule, but we still must obey each one.

When we break the law out of rebellion and disregard for authority, it's an embarrassment to God. Even if we don't technically break the law, we can still cause much grief by badmouthing the authorities God has placed over us. A few loose-lipped Christians can cause others to view Christianity as harsh and judgmental, and who wants to be a part of *that*? God wants us to submit, with respect, to those He has placed in positions of authority. Do it for *His* sake.

Dear Father, remind me to honor You by honoring authority. Amen.

IN THE WAIT

For no one is cast off by the Lord forever.
Though He brings grief, he will show
compassion, so great is his unfailing love.

LAMENTATIONS 3:31–32 NIV

When life is hard and we find ourselves in difficult circumstances, it's easy to feel like God has forgotten us. We live in a fast-food society, and we expect our prayers to be answered quickly, with time to spare. We get frustrated when God doesn't respond in a prompt and efficient manner.

God doesn't live by our timetable. He knows that growth happens during the wait time. He wants us to be happy; but even more, He wants us to be strong and mature in our faith. So sometimes, He makes us wait. And wait and wait.

But the wait will not last forever. God loves us. He hears our prayers, and He counts every tear. Keep seeking Him, and don't give up. His compassion is boundless, and His love for you is beyond measure.

Dear Father, please hear my prayers and answer me quickly. While I'm waiting for You to act, help my faith grow stronger. I trust in Your unfailing love. Amen.

RICH IN SPIRIT

It is the blessing of the LORD that makes
rich, and He adds no sorrow to it.
PROVERBS 10:22 NASB

For many things, we Christians have the same vocabulary as the rest of the world. But there's a problem with that—we use different dictionaries. And when the same word is used to describe two entirely different things, confusion follows.

The word *rich* is a perfect example. To the world, *rich* means monetary wealth. But in God's dictionary, *rich* means an abundance in treasures, such as peace, love, joy, compassion, kindness, and contentment. God's definition is much more powerful than the world's, for monetary wealth cannot eliminate feelings of sorrow, rejection, or failure.

When we totally rely on God, He makes us rich in spirit. And that kind of wealth overshadows, and often eliminates, our deepest sorrows.

Dear Father, thank You for making me rich in
spirit. Remind me to measure my life and my
riches by Your standards, not the world's. I know
the wealth that comes from You is far greater
than a sizable bank account. Amen.

A STRONGHOLD

The LORD is my light and my salvation—
whom shall I fear? The LORD is the stronghold
of my life—of whom shall I be afraid?

PSALM 27:1 NIV

Fear is a prison—dark, cold, and tight. Every person has experienced the stifling confinement of fear at one time or another. We may be afraid of failure, rejection, illness, or something else. Whatever our fear, we have a way of escape. Our relationship with God will set us free, if we let it.

Where fear brings gloom, God brings light to overpower the darkness. Where fear makes us cold, His light offers warmth. And where fear confines us, God's light sets us free.

The psalmist calls the Lord his stronghold. In other words, God has a grip on our lives, and He will not let us go. No matter our circumstances, we can relax knowing God has surrounded us with the fortress of His love, the castle of His protection. We are His, and we are ever in His care. We have *nothing* to be afraid of.

Dear Father, thank You for keeping Your grip on
my life. Remind me not to be afraid. Amen.

FINDING THE RIGHT JOB

*So I saw that there is nothing better for a person than
to enjoy their work, because that is their lot. For who
can bring them to see what will happen after them?*

ECCLESIASTES 3:22 NIV

Work can be a source of great fulfillment or immense
stress. While any job has pressure and difficulty at
times, we should try to find work we enjoy. If we
dread going to work each day and lose sleep at night
over our jobs, we should consider finding another
job or line of work.

Work is supposed to help us sleep *better*, not keep
us from resting. It's supposed to provide us with a
boosted self-esteem and sense of purpose. If we're
struggling in the workplace, we should first make
sure we're giving our best effort to our employer. If
we are, and we're still not happy, perhaps it's time
to search for other options. God wants us to be
happy in our work.

*Dear Father, You created me. You know my
heart, my gifts, my talents. Please help me find
employment that matches my talents and my
preferences. I want to be happy in my work. Amen.*

RECIPE FOR CHRISTIAN LIVING

*Be joyful in hope, patient in
affliction, faithful in prayer.*
ROMANS 12:12 NIV

This verse contains a recipe for successful Christian living. The first ingredient is hope, which we are to cling to with joy. The two go hand in hand, really. When we realize the hope—or the promise of good things—we have in Christ, we can't help but feel joy in our hearts.

The second ingredient is patience, which we apply through all the afflictions we encounter. Our human nature urges us to be short tempered and difficult during tough times, but God wants us to show patience even when it's hard. He wants us to wait for His perfect timing and trust Him.

Finally, we add the most important ingredient, which is prayer. We are to pray continually. God wants to be involved in every moment of our lives. When we include each of these three ingredients, we will find strength and joy and peace in His presence.

*Dear Father, thank You for this recipe for godly
living. Help me to include each ingredient in
my life, in the correct amounts. Amen.*

NOTHING TO FEAR

He got up, rebuked the wind and said to the waves,
"Quiet! Be still!" Then the wind died down and it
was completely calm. He said to his disciples, "Why
are you so afraid? Do you still have no faith?"

MARK 4:39–40 NIV

The disciples were afraid the storm would overtake them. They didn't understand how Jesus could be so calm—and even sleep—through such a torrent. Jesus showed them they had nothing to fear. He had it all under control.

On that day, theirs was a physical storm. In our lives, we face storms of many kinds. Sometimes, it feels like God is sleeping, like He doesn't care about the issues we're facing. Just as Jesus commanded the weather and it obeyed Him, God has dominion over every circumstance in our lives. He loves us; and if He seems absent, it may be because He knows we have nothing to fear. He's not concerned, because He's already taken care of our every need.

When we're afraid, we can picture God commanding our situations: "Quiet! Be still!" We can trust Him, trust His power, and trust His everlasting love for us.

Dear Father, I trust You. Amen.

CONSTANT, LOVING DISCIPLINE

*Folly is bound up in the heart of a child, but
the rod of discipline will drive it far away.*
PROVERBS 22:15 NIV

Many people mistakenly believe this verse is about
corporal punishment. Volumes have been written
about whether using the rod—or spanking—is an
appropriate punishment. Whichever side of the
fence you're on, we all must agree that this verse is
about the need for discipline.

Every one of us is born with a tendency to sin. It's in
our nature. We are self-centered, self-absorbed, greedy
people. Discipline, or consistent training, helps to shape
us into selfless, other-centered, generous people. That
kind of transformation will never occur on its own. It is
only brought about by persistent teaching.

Parenting is a long, exhausting job; and at times
it's easy to ignore the adorable, nasty little habits that
young ones develop. But if we don't discipline our
children, other people won't like them when they're
adults. When we discipline with constant, loving
diligence, we shape and grow caring, successful
people who are loved and beloved.

*Dear Father, help me discipline my child
with consistency and love. Amen.*

REACH OUT IN FAITH

*Jesus turned, and seeing her he said, "Take
heart, daughter; your faith has made you well."
And instantly the woman was made well.*

MATTHEW 9:22 ESV

This woman might be categorized in our society as a feminist. In a world where women had few rights and were treated as second-class citizens, this woman had the gumption to help herself. For twelve years, she had bled without stopping. She was considered unclean. She was an outcast. And yet she pushed her way through the crowd to the Healer, to the one person she knew could help her.

When all hope seems lost, when others discount us and treat us like we're losers and we don't matter, we can learn from this woman. We can push ourselves up, dust ourselves off, and do what we must to help ourselves. And the most important thing we can do, which will bring the best results, is go to Christ. Reach out to Him, knowing He is the one who can help us. He will look at us and say, "Take heart. Your faith has healed you."

*Dear Father, I reach out to You in faith.
I need You to help me. Amen.*

TRUST HIS HEART

He sent out his word and healed them,
and delivered them from their destruction.
PSALM 107:20 ESV

When we think of healing, we usually think of our physical health. But healing takes many shapes and forms. Sometimes we pray for physical healing for our loved ones or ourselves, but God wants to work an even greater miracle. He wants to heal our spirits. He wants to deliver us from destruction.

What if, in His great mercy, God knows that physical wholeness will lead us on an even greater path of destruction? What if our loved one is physically ill but emotionally healthy, and *we're* the ones who need spiritual healing? What if that physical ailment brings us closer to Him, keeps us clinging to Him in a way that would never happen if all were well?

God wants to heal us of our diseases. But even more, He wants to deliver us from destruction. We need to trust His love for us, knowing He has our very best interest in His heart, every moment.

Dear Father, I trust You. Please heal me
of whatever needs healing. Amen.

SHARING THE LOAD

*Two are better than one, because they
have a good return for their labor.*

ECCLESIASTES 4:9 NIV

One reason God created work is to connect us to other people. Most jobs have, as their purpose, a way to help others, provide a service for others, or offer a product that will enhance others' lives. God is all about relationships.

When we try to Lone-Ranger our way through our jobs, we find a lowered level of job satisfaction. Even introverts need connections. When we connect with others and help each other find success in our employment, we feel energized. We laugh more, smile more, and increase our productivity.

Instead of worrying about how we can amplify our own sense of satisfaction in our jobs, perhaps we can focus on helping someone else find more satisfaction. Building relationships and sharing the load will increase our job output and the sense of fulfillment we find in our own work.

*Dear Father, help me help somebody in their
work today. Place partners in my life with
whom I can share the workload. Amen.*

GOD SEES. . .HE HEARS

I called on your name, LORD, from the
depths of the pit. You heard my plea: "Do
not close your ears to my cry for relief."
LAMENTATIONS 3:55–56 NIV

Do you ever feel like your prayers aren't going any higher than the ceiling? Sometimes, it seems we're sinking deeper and deeper into a bottomless pit, and our cries for help aren't even making it to the surface.

But God hears. He leans forward to listen; He eagerly waits for us to seek Him, to cry out for Him. The most precious sound in the world to Him must be the sound of one of His beloved children calling His name.

In the midst of the deepest, darkest troubles, we can be confident that God sees. He hears. And in the silence, in the wait time, He is actively working to weave every circumstance together for our good.

Dear Father, sometimes it feels like You're
not listening, but I know that's not true.
Please hear me. Let me feel the evidence of
Your presence today. I love You, I trust You,
and I know You are good. Amen.

A TIGHT GRIP

And God is able to make all grace abound to you,
so that always having all sufficiency in everything,
you may have an abundance for every good deed.

2 CORINTHIANS 9:8 NASB

When we're strapped for money or resources, our first instinct is often to grip what we have a little tighter. If we're not careful, we can become stingy with the blessings God has given us. But God is a generous God, and He wants His children to be generous as well.

God gives us more than we need. He doesn't give us an abundance so we can hoard it and buy more temporary stuff. He likes to see us happy, and it's not wrong to purchase things to make our lives better—as long as our own comfort doesn't stand in front of our generosity.

God will supply our needs. In turn, He wants us to supply others' needs. When we follow this principle of generous giving, we'll often find we have enough left over to supply our wants as well as our needs.

Dear Father, teach me to be
generous, like You. Amen.

SURROUNDED BY COMFORT

Praise be to the God and Father of our Lord Jesus Christ, the Father of compassion and the God of all comfort, who comforts us in all our troubles, so that we can comfort those in any trouble with the comfort we ourselves receive from God.

2 CORINTHIANS 1:3–4 NIV

We all like to feel comfortable, or surrounded with comfort. When we're comfortable, we are relaxed and contented in God's presence, despite our circumstances. God is full of compassion, and when we're going through a difficult time, we can be assured He is right there, waiting, wanting to comfort us.

We are His messengers on this earth. Because He cares for us so tenderly, He wants us to turn around and care for others. We are to offer comfort and compassion to people who are hurting. When we do that, the blessings are twofold: the people we comfort receive a taste of God's goodness; and we are comforted as well! God knows that when we focus our hearts on caring for others, we forget our own troubles for a time.

Dear Father, thank You for Your comfort. Help me comfort others in need. Amen.

WITH ALL YOUR MIGHT

*Whatever your hand finds to do, do it with
all your might, for in the realm of the dead,
where you are going, there is neither working
nor planning nor knowledge nor wisdom.*

ECCLESIASTES 9:10 NIV

God gave us the ability to do all kinds of things. But one thing we can't do is turn back time. Once a day is gone, it's gone. That's why it's important to make the most of our time when we have it.

Whatever we're doing, God wants us to give our whole selves to that. If we're in a business meeting but secretly texting our best friends under the table, we're not giving our whole selves to that meeting. If we're working on the computer but allowing social media distractions, we're not giving our whole selves to our work. The day will end, and we may wonder why we didn't accomplish more.

Look around. When something needs doing, do it! Do it with all your might, until the job is complete. Then, when the day is over, you'll feel a sense of accomplishment for a task well done.

Dear Father, help me to focus and work hard. Amen.

WHAT IS RIGHT

Don't depend on your own wisdom. Respect the
LORD and refuse to do wrong. Then your body
will be healthy, and your bones will be strong.

PROVERBS 3:7–8 NCV

Sometimes, what *feels* right isn't necessarily what *is*
right. When we want something, it's easy to reason
it out in our minds. Reliance on our own wisdom
can get us into trouble.

God's wisdom will never let us down. Though
living by His principles often *feels* contrary to our
sinful nature, we can be sure that God's ways will
always lead us down a path of life and peace and a
deep, inner joy that cannot be matched.

If it's immediate gratification we're seeking, then
our own wisdom is the way to go. But if we long
for long-term health—physical, emotional, and
spiritual—then we need to set aside what *feels*
right, if it's contrary to God's Word, and do what
is right.

Dear Father, help me follow Your wisdom and
not my own. I trust You, and I know You will lead
me on the very best path for my life. Amen.

A CLOSE WATCH

*A rod and a reprimand impart wisdom, but a
child left undisciplined disgraces its mother.*
PROVERBS 29:15 NIV

A shepherd has a tough job. Sheep tend to wander, and the shepherd's job is to keep the sheep in line and to keep them safe. When left on their own, the sheep will surely wander into danger or get lost on the wrong path.

We humans are similar to sheep. When left to our own wisdom and desires, we'll surely stray down the wrong path. We'll get lost, make poor choices, and bring shame on the people we love.

So it only stands to reason that as parents, we need to keep a close watch on our children. We need to teach them, train them, and discipline them. When we leave them to make their own choices too soon and too often, they will certainly give in to the sin nature, which will cause heartache and destruction. Consistent teaching and reproof leads to wise choices.

*Dear Father, thank You for Your loving discipline
in my life. Help me offer the same type of love
and correction to my own children. Amen.*

POUR INTO RELATIONSHIPS

But Martha was distracted by all the preparations
that had to be made. She came to him and asked,
"Lord, don't you care that my sister has left me
to do the work by myself? Tell her to help me!"

LUKE 10:40 NIV

We live in a *Martha* world. Thousands—possibly millions—of books have been written to help us increase our productivity. When Martha felt like her sister had left her with all the work, she became agitated—and understandably so.

Though God admires hard work and a job well done, His priority is always, *always* relationships. What Martha didn't realize was that Mary had, in that moment, made a better choice. Mary chose to sit at Jesus' feet, listen to His stories, and pour her attention into that relationship.

God is pleased when we work hard. He is not pleased, however, when we value work over people. We were created to connect with other people. Sometimes we need to make a judgment call, lay down our tools, and pour time and attention into our relationships.

Dear Father, give me wisdom to see when to
work, and when to build a relationship. Amen.

WHEN HOPE GROWS THIN

"Do not work for food that spoils, but for food that endures to eternal life, which the Son of Man will give you. For on him God the Father has placed his seal of approval."

JOHN 6:27 NIV

When money is scarce and we don't know where the next meal will come from, it's easy to become discouraged. During those times, we can lose hope. Yet it's during life's hardest trials that we often feel God's most overpowering presence. When hope grows thin, God is strong. He is present. And He is good.

It's difficult not to let fear and anxiety rule our hearts, especially when things aren't going the way we want them to. But God wants us to trust Him! When we choose faith and hope, even during trials. . . when we continue to work to please our heavenly Father, He sees, and He places a seal of approval on our lives. Hang in there. Blessings are on the way.

Dear Father, remind me of Your presence. I want to trust You, please You, and live for You. Amen.

MAKING PEACE

When the LORD takes pleasure in anyone's way,
he causes their enemies to make peace with them.

PROVERBS 16:7 NIV

Wouldn't it be great if every enemy we had decided they wanted to live at peace with us? What a glorious existence that would be! God's Word tells us that it's possible. When we live our lives to please God—when our thoughts and actions are governed by what makes Him happy—He will bless us. And one of the ways He blesses us is by causing our enemies to make peace with us.

That doesn't necessarily mean our enemies will become our best friends or that we'll be one big happy family. There will always be differences of opinion and lifestyles. But when we live to please God—which includes being a peacemaker—we are able to live and let live. God causes our enemies to back off, leave us alone, and go about their business without disrupting our peace.

Dear Father, I want to please You, and I
want to live at peace with my enemies.
Show me how to do my part. Amen.

CALL ON HIM

You came near when I called you,
and you said, "Do not fear."
LAMENTATIONS 3:57 NIV

God promised never to leave us nor forsake us. But sometimes it feels like He's a million miles away. When troubles threaten to overwhelm us, it may seem like God's taken an extended vacation. We feel forgotten. We feel scared and alone.

When we call on Him, He comes as close as a breath, as near as our own heartbeat. In response to our desperate pleas for His presence, He whispers, "Hush, child. Don't be afraid. I'm right here."

Does He feel far away? Call Him. Call Him again and again, until His presence fills the space you occupy. Call Him, and listen for His response. He is there, holding you in His arms, pulling you into His lap, and comforting you.

Dear Father, I know You promised never to leave
me, but right now I can't feel Your presence. It
seems like You've forgotten me. I'm afraid, and
I feel alone. Please come; I need You. Amen.

MORE BLESSED TO GIVE

"In everything I did, I showed you that by this
kind of hard work we must help the weak,
remembering the words the Lord Jesus himself
said: 'It is more blessed to give than to receive.'"

ACTS 20:35 NIV

It's frustrating when we feel like we carry more than our share of the load. God designed us *all* to work hard, and sometimes we work harder than those around us. When we feel others are benefiting from our sweat-inducing labor, resentment can creep up.

But that resentment quickly fades when we look at things the way Paul instructs us to. Isn't it better to be the strong one? Isn't it better to be the one with surplus—the one with something to give? How much harder would it be if we weren't able to work because we're physically, mentally, or emotionally weak?

The ability to work is a blessing. The ability to give to others and to carry a heavier portion of the burden—because we're strong—is an even greater gift. Generosity to others is a privilege, not a curse.

Dear Father, thank You for opportunities to
work hard and share with others. Amen.

WALK IN FAITH AND WISDOM

So that the tested genuineness of your faith—more precious than gold that perishes though it is tested by fire—may be found to result in praise and glory and honor at the revelation of Jesus Christ.

1 PETER 1:7 ESV

One characteristic of wisdom is the ability to see beyond. It's the knack for looking past the here and now and knowing what lies in the future. Like salt and pepper, faith and wisdom are a matched set.

When we lack faith and wisdom, our actions serve us right here, right now. But without foresight, we'll find ourselves at the end of our lives with little to show for our labor. With faith, we know the best is yet to come. When we walk in faith, we walk knowing that at the end of this journey, great rewards wait for us.

Dear Father, I know You have amazing things in store for me. Give me wisdom to push aside the things that distract me, and help me walk in faith toward the ultimate goal of pleasing You. Amen.

CONFIDENCE IN THE PROVIDER

"But blessed is the one who trusts in the LORD,
whose confidence is in him. They will be like a
tree planted by the water that sends out its roots
by the stream. It does not fear when heat comes;
its leaves are always green. It has no worries in a
year of drought and never fails to bear fruit."

JEREMIAH 17:7–8 NIV

We all go through times of financial drought. These are the times we have more money going out than coming in. During a drought, our first instinct is often to worry and stress about the future.

But blessed are those who trust in the Lord, who've made the Lord their hope and confidence. Who needs the rain when we have God? When we are firmly positioned in Him, in His Word, in His promises, we have a source that goes deep and will never run dry. When we place our confidence in God as our provider, we will continue to be productive, even when our finances feel parched.

Dear Father, when it comes to my finances—
and everything else in my life—I place all
my hope and confidence in You. Amen.

HIGHER WAYS

We work hard with our own hands.
When we are cursed, we bless; when
we are persecuted, we endure it.

1 CORINTHIANS 4:12 NIV

Sometimes, what God expects of us doesn't make any sense. It goes against every ounce of human nature. After all, it's only natural to curse someone who curses us. It's only normal to fight back when others persecute us.

Yet God's ways are higher than our ways. Though His wisdom may seem unnatural, it will always lead to more peace and more satisfaction in our lives. God sees everything, and He will take vengeance on the unjust. He doesn't want us to concern ourselves with that. He wants us to return hate with love. He wants us to return cruelty with kindness. And God, who knows all, will reward our consistent hard work and purity of heart, and bring about much better justice than we could imagine.

> *Dear Father, please help me to work hard*
> *and show humility. I trust You to take*
> *care of injustice as You see fit. Amen.*

SCRIPTURAL PRINCIPLES

Out of the same mouth come praise and cursing.
My brothers and sisters, this should not be.
JAMES 3:10 NIV

Have you ever known a two-faced person? Like it or not, we all have a tendency to be a little two-faced, if we're not careful. We smile to a person's face and whisper negative things behind their back. James warns us against such behavior. It's wrong. It causes hurt feelings and broken relationships.

When dealing with others, we need to employ the principles taught in scripture. We don't need to let any unwholesome, negative talk come from our mouths, but only what is helpful for building others up (Ephesians 4:29). When we do confront someone, we should do it privately, with a loving and gentle spirit. But being friendly to someone's face and gossiping about that person behind their back is not the way God's children are called to act. If we need to pour our frustrations out, we can always do so on our knees—to our heavenly Father who hears, who knows, and who cares.

Dear Father, help me to know when to speak
the truth in love and when to remain silent.
I don't want to be two-faced. Amen.

STAYING CLOSE

The LORD is close to the brokenhearted and
saves those who are crushed in spirit. The
righteous person may have many troubles,
but the LORD delivers him from them all.

PSALM 34:18–19 NIV

When our hearts are broken and our spirits crushed, we can know without doubt that God is right there with us. He cries with us. He aches with us. He cannot stay away from us when we are hurting, for His passion is for us.

God's Word never promises an easy life. Trouble will follow us whether we live for God or not. We are assured, however, that if we follow God—if we live for Him—He will never leave us to trudge through our hardships alone. When we feel lonely, we can simply breathe in. His presence is right there, filling every breath, pounding with every heartbeat. He will walk with us each painful step of the way, and He will deliver us to a place of hope and joy and peace.

Dear Father, thank You for staying close to
me. Help me feel Your presence. Amen.

GOD FIRST

*But Peter and the apostles answered,
"We must obey God rather than men."*
ACTS 5:29 NASB

Time and again, God asks us to respect the law and honor authority. There is one exception to that rule. If the government or our employer asks us to choose them over God, we're exempt. We should always, *always* choose God.

Most times, we honor authority by showing up on time, by following the rules (even if we disagree with them), and by showing public respect, if not support. But when we're faced with a choice between God and government, our faith or our paycheck, God comes first. Even if that choice costs us our lives, we must still choose God. We already know how the story ends—we win. We will spend eternity with Him in heaven.

Most choices are not nearly so high stakes. When our preferences are pitted against our authority, we should honor those in authority. But when it's a choice of faith against favor, we should always choose faith.

*Dear Father, give me wisdom to know when
to submit and when to fight. Amen.*

171

NEVER FRUITLESS!

Therefore, my dear brothers and sisters, stand firm. Let nothing move you. Always give yourselves fully to the work of the Lord, because you know that your labor in the Lord is not in vain.

1 CORINTHIANS 15:58 NIV

When something is done in vain, that means it's pointless. Fruitless. It has no purpose and no lasting results. When we work and work, and we feel like we're not getting anywhere, it can feel like our work is in vain.

But work done for the Lord is never fruitless! God's timing is different from ours, and we may not see fruits as quickly as we'd like. But anytime we work hard, with pleasing God as our goal, our work will not be in vain. God sees, He knows, and He will reward those who give their hearts—and their subsequent actions—to Him.

> *Dear Father, sometimes I feel like giving up. Sometimes it feels like my hard work is not accomplishing the things I need to accomplish. Yet I love You; You have my heart. I will keep going—for You. Amen.*

CHRIST IS FOR US

You, Lord, took up my case; you redeemed my life.
LAMENTATIONS 3:58 NIV

In 1 John chapter 2, Christ is referred to as our advocate, or our mediator. In other words, He is our lawyer, defending our cause. Hundreds of years before Christ walked the earth, Jeremiah used the same word picture. Like a lawyer, God has taken up our case and passionately works on our behalf.

Though circumstances may threaten to overwhelm us, we can relax, for God is both lawyer and judge. He loves us. He is always for us, never against us. It doesn't matter what kind of trouble we're in or how we got into our current situation. He has our ultimate good as His goal, and He works tirelessly to bring about His beautiful purpose in our lives.

Dear Father, thank You for this reminder that You are my advocate. You have taken up my case, and You are working right now on my behalf. I trust You, and I know that somehow You will redeem this situation for my good and for Your purpose. Amen.

HEART GIVING

*Give generously to them and do so without
a grudging heart; then because of this the
Lord your God will bless you in all your work
and in everything you put your hand to.*

Deuteronomy 15:10 niv

When finances are tight, it's easy to put giving to God at the bottom of the list. We pay our other bills first; and if there's anything left, we'll give that to God. Maybe.

Or we go ahead and give to God first, but we don't like it. We grumble. We think, *If I didn't have to give my tithe, I'd have enough left to pay for other, more important things.* We may not admit we feel this way; but if we examine our hearts, we'll often find a little resentment over what we give to God.

God doesn't need our money. He *wants* our hearts. When we take joy in whatever we give to God, He is delighted. When we give generously to Him, with love and excitement over the gift, He will bless us.

Dear Father, I may not have much to give, but I want to give everything I can. I love You. Amen.

PEACE IN THE STORM

And he said to them, "Why are you afraid,
O you of little faith?" Then he rose and rebuked
the winds and the sea, and there was a great calm.
MATTHEW 8:26 ESV

If we look back over our lives, we can see God's hand at work. We can see that, no matter how bad things might have been, God was right there with us, steering our ship and keeping us safe. But stories of God's goodness go much further than our own lives. Throughout history, God has shown Himself faithful to our parents and grandparents, to all our ancestors—all the way back through biblical times and to the beginning of time.

So why do we question Him? Why do we look at our current storms and feel afraid? When we find ourselves having little faith, we can remind ourselves of our stories and the stories of those before us, and we will find peace.

Dear Father, forgive me for my lack of
faith. Please remind me of Your power,
and calm my storm. Amen.

WILLING AND HUMBLE

For even when we were with you, we
gave you this rule: "The one who is
unwilling to work shall not eat."

2 Thessalonians 3:10 niv

Some may question this verse as showing a lack of compassion for the hungry. However, this verse doesn't refer to those who are unable to work. Paul clearly states that he's talking about those who are *unwilling* to work. God created us in His image; He made us for work.

When we are ill, or circumstances beyond our control prevent us from working, God sees. He will provide for His children who *want* to work, but who are not able. But when we are lazy—when we choose not to work because we'd rather let others carry the load—God is not pleased. God wants us to be willing and humble enough to do what needs to be done, so we can have the self-respect that comes from working for our food and our other needs.

Dear Father, I am willing to work. Please
provide me with the right job. Amen.

CLING TO HIM

God is within her, she will not fall;
God will help her at break of day.

PSALM 46:5 NIV

Depression's voice seems to speak louder at night. We lie awake, listening to thoughts about how low we are or how bad things could get. We feel helpless and without hope, and are certain we will fail.

If we quiet our souls and really listen, we'll know God is there, whispering His love, His hope, and His help. He is right within our hearts; and if we cling to Him, He'll hold us up. He won't let us fall under the weight of our depression.

Psalm 30:5 tells us that sorrow may last through the night, but joy comes in the morning. In the verse above, the psalmist assures us that if we can just hang in there until daybreak, God will make His presence known, and He will see us through another day.

Dear Father, thank You for Your promise
to help me and hold me up. Thank You for
new days and new beginnings. Amen.

OUR DEFENDER

*LORD, you have seen the wrong
done to me. Uphold my cause!*

LAMENTATIONS 3:59 NIV

One of the most frequently asked questions, when it comes to matters of faith, is *why?* Why does God allow bad things to happen to people who love Him?

It is a difficult question without an easy answer. The truth is, God *could* prevent bad things from happening. But He wants us to have freedom to choose, right or wrong.

With that freedom comes risk. One poor choice has a ripple effect, causing bad things to happen to us and those around us. If I choose to smoke cigarettes, I may get cancer, which will hurt me. It will also break the hearts of all who love me. By giving us freedom of choice, God chooses to allow the consequences of those choices.

He sees every choice made and every wrong done. He is compassionate, and He is just. He may not prevent bad things from happening, but He will defend our cause.

*Dear Father, thank You for
upholding my cause. Amen.*

WORK AND LOVE

*God is not unjust; he will not forget your work
and the love you have shown him as you have
helped his people and continue to help them.*

HEBREWS 6:10 NIV

At some point, everyone wonders about his or her
purpose in life. But God's Word makes it pretty clear
what our purpose is: we're here to love. Period. We
were created to love God and to love other people.

The work we do is one of the most important
ways we show love. It is through our work that we
help others. It is through our work that we take
care of our families. Whatever we do—whether it's
cleaning up after others, providing a service, or
helping others reach their full potential—we should
have love as our primary goal. When our love for
God continuously spills into our relationships with
others, God is pleased, and He will make sure we
are rewarded.

*Dear Father, remind me today—and every
day—that my work is a way to show love
to You and other people. Amen.*

DRAW NEAR

*Let us then with confidence draw near to the
throne of grace, that we may receive mercy
and find grace to help in time of need.*

HEBREWS 4:16 ESV

When we feel our faith slipping away, we often look around in confusion, wondering where our confidence in God has gone. Faith seems elusive; it's there one day and gone the next. But if we're honest with ourselves, we'll realize that God hasn't moved. He is always right on His throne. If we feel far from Him, we're the ones who moved.

When our faith needs strengthening, all we need to do is draw near to God. We'll find the confidence we need, along with every bit of mercy and grace to see us through each day, when we stand as close as we can to our Father.

We draw near by reading His Word, praying, and listening for His response. When we consistently do those things, we'll find our faith is strong, and we feel the peace and inner joy He promised.

*Dear Father, forgive me for ever leaving Your side.
I want to draw near to You. Thank You for always
welcoming me into Your presence. Amen.*

DISCIPLINE AND DELIGHT

*Discipline your children, and they will give you
peace; they will bring you the delights you desire.*
PROVERBS 29:17 NIV

The words *discipline* and *delight* are seldom thought
of in the same sentence. Discipline is hard work.
It's a commitment to do the same thing, again and
again and again until the lesson is learned, the task
accomplished. Discipline is often more of a drudge
than a delight. But the *result* of consistent discipline
is a beautiful thing. The act of discipline will bring
about the result of rest for our spirits and delight
to our hearts.

Just as a disciplined athlete can hope for that
moment of glory when a medal is placed around his
or her neck, the parent who is steadfast in teaching
and training must keep the end goal in mind. Someday, when all the lessons are learned, that child's
character will bring us joy, delight, and peace.

*Dear Father, help me to stay the course when
it comes to loving discipline for my children.
Remind me to keep the end goal in mind. Amen.*

PERFECT PEACE

*"You keep him in perfect peace whose mind is
stayed on you, because he trusts in you."*

ISAIAH 26:3 ESV

Trust is tricky, even with those we can see and touch.
Placing our trust in God, whom we can't see, can
feel impossible. When trust in God isn't easy, we
need to remind ourselves of a few history lessons.

When an enormous sea stood between the
Israelites and safety, God parted the sea. When
five thousand people were hungry, Christ fed them
with one small basket of food. Time and again, in
God's Word, we are told how God came through in
times of trouble.

When we look back at our own lives, if we're honest with ourselves, we will see God's handprints all
over our history. We have a fender bender that could
have been a fatal crash. We find a much-needed
dress for an event, on the clearance rack, 75 percent
off. We receive an unexpected sum of money when
we thought all hope was lost.

Trusting God makes sense. When we place our
trust in God, He will meet our needs, and we will
have peace.

*Dear Father, I trust You. Thank
You for Your peace. Amen.*

AN ALIVE FAITH

*What does it profit, my brethren, if someone
says he has faith but does not have works? Can
faith save him? If a brother or sister is naked and
destitute of daily food, and one of you says to
them, "Depart in peace, be warmed and filled,"
but you do not give them the things which are
needed for the body, what does it profit? Thus also
faith by itself, if it does not have works, is dead.*
JAMES 2:14–17 NKJV

When we hear people talk about their faith, but
their actions don't match their words, it can be a
little nauseating. Deep down, whether we've actually considered it or not, we all know that faith
is best shown through actions. That's why James
points out to us that faith that's not accompanied
by works is dead. When our faith feels dead, one
of the quickest ways to revive it is to simply get
busy doing God's work.

*Dear Father, I want my faith to be alive. Show me
ways to make my actions match my words. Amen.*

GOOD THINGS

That is why we labor and strive, because we have put our hope in the living God, who is the Savior of all people, and especially of those who believe.

1 TIMOTHY 4:10 NIV

There's quite possibly no worse feeling in the world than the feeling of lost hope. Since hope is the belief that good things will happen in the future, lost hope reflects a conviction that nothing good is left. No matter what, only bad things will come.

That's a pretty sad way to exist.

When we have Christ, we have hope. We have the internal assurance that no matter how bad things get, good things are on the way! God loves us, and He is always working on our behalf to give us hope, peace, and joy. And at the end of it all, we will have eternal life in His presence.

Because of this hope, we can keep going. We can keep working, striving, and pressing on. No matter what happens today, we can know beyond doubt—good things are on the way.

Dear Father, thank You for the promise of good things. Thank You for hope. Amen.

SCRIPTURE INDEX